Estes

ENGLISH HERB GARDENS

ENGLISH HERB GARDENS

GUY COOPER AND GORDON TAYLOR

PHOTOGRAPHS BY
CLIVE BOURSNELL

FOREWORD BY
ROSEMARY VEREY

RIZZOLI
NEW YORK

First published in the United States of America in 1986 by
RIZZOLI INTERNATIONAL PUBLICATIONS, INC.
597 Fifth Avenue, New York, NY 10017

First published in Great Britain in 1986 by
George Weidenfeld & Nicolson Ltd

Library of Congress Cataloging-in-Publication Data

Cooper, Guy.
   English herb gardens.

   Bibliography: p.
   Includes index.
   1. Herb gardens—England.   1. Taylor, Gordon
(Gordon I.) II. Title.
SB351.H5C66   1986   635'.7'0942   85–43480
ISBN 0–8478–0689–8

Designed by Joyce Chester

Colour separations by Newsele Litho Ltd
Filmset by Keyspools Ltd, Golborne, Lancashire
Printed and bound in Italy by L.E.G.O., Vicenza

Half Title Page Stockheld Park, Wetherby, North Yorkshire
Title Page The Tudor House, Southampton, Hampshire
Overleaf Hestercombe House, Cheddon Fitzpaine, Somerset

AUTHORS' ACKNOWLEDGMENTS

WE GRATEFULLY THANK all of the owners of the 180 herb gardens we visited without any prior notice; with few exceptions they were most helpful and patient. These initial reconnaissance trips were made particularly effective and pleasant through the efforts of Mrs Rosemary Verey, Mrs Sarah Garland, Elizabeth and Reginald Peplow and the staff of The Herb Society. Special thanks are due to them and to many other friends who gave both help and hospitality: Mr John Bedford, Lady Caroline Blois, Ronald and Elizabeth Cowie, Mr Godfrey Holden, Mrs Irene Milburn, Mrs Louise Pleydell-Bouverie, the late Alisdair Orr and Caroline Orr, Mrs Rosemary Titterington and Elizabeth and James van den Bergh. We must thank also our several temporary secretaries.

Our penultimate thanks are to Mr Michael Dover and Miss Felicity Luard, Director and Managing Editor of Weidenfeld and Nicolson's illustrated books.

Our ultimate thanks are to Mr Clive Boursnell for his obsessive, Byronic energy and for pertinaciously living in his camper van for nine weeks in order to take the photographs, which capture an essence of each of the herb gardens shown here.

6

CONTENTS

Authors' Acknowledgments
5

Foreword by Rosemary Verey
9

Introduction
13

The Gardens
19

A Glossary of Herbs
134

Gardens Open to the Public
155

Photographer's Notes and Acknowledgments
156

Select Bibliography
158

Index
159

FOREWORD

by Rosemary Verey

O<small>N REFLECTION</small> I do not think that there has been a period in garden history when the herb garden has played a more important role both in garden design and in the use of herbs for cooking than it does today.

In medieval monastic gardens the culinary herbs were grown among the vegetables, while the physic herbs were cultivated in a separate plot by the monk in charge of the infirmary. They were grown in individual, narrow, parallel, rectangular beds for ease of picking and in the case of the medicinal herbs to help prevent unfortunate mistakes in administering the wrong remedy.

How I would love to be transported into a scented Elizabethan garden with herbs and Honeysuckles, a knot garden and Roses clambering over a simple arbour, or 'roosting place' as one contemporary writer called it. There was a romantic sense about garden-making then; it was a peaceful though dynamic time when country ladies and their gentlemen created beautiful surroundings to their newly built manor houses. In so doing they broke away from the formula of straight monastic beds, using attractive patterns and designs.

For them the word 'herb' had a wider connotation than it does today. William Lawson wrote in the sixteenth century, 'herbs are of two sorts, therefore it is meet that we have two gardens: a garden for flowers and a kitchen garden.' From the flower garden Roses and Lavender 'yield much profit and comfort to the senses'. The housewife could use these in her still-room to make Lavender and Rose water for 'reviving the spirits by the sense of smell'.

The still-room continued but the herb garden became less important with the advent of the landscape garden. Curiously, during Victorian times little culinary use was made of herbs.

Early in this century there was a definite revival in the use of herbs and

Barnsley House, Barnsley,
Gloucestershire

9

consequently in re-discovering the enchantment of making a garden full of scents and plants for herbal receipts and potpourri. Vita Sackville-West at Sissinghurst inspired gardeners with her writing and with the herb garden she created; her garden has been the inspiration behind many that have been made in the ensuing fifty years. She gathered the scented plants from around the beds and borders and put them together with the culinary herbs to create a garden both beautiful and useful. From this moment we have become increasingly aware of the joy of having a special place for our herbs and scented plants.

Who better than Guy Cooper and Gordon Taylor to take up the story and to tell us about the herb gardens they have discovered as they travelled round England? The authors were for six and a half years the joint co-directors of The Herb Society of Great Britain and have visited herb gardens all over the country. They present this selection of gardens in an original manner giving some of the history of each place together with just enough description to inspire prospective herb-garden makers to see as many as possible before launching into their own project.

The gardens range from the smallest to the largest, from the herb garden at Peterborough Cathedral designed by Elizabeth Peplow where only plants known and grown in 1302 have been used, to Acorn Bank where one can see the most interesting medicinal garden. There is a herb farm in central Birmingham, and at Kilmersdon near Bath the neat display garden demonstrates how easy it is to create a mature effect in only two years. What becomes apparent in this book is the diversity of styles, shapes and sizes; there are ideas for every gardener who is planning a herb garden and particular pleasure for people planning a garden tour, combining history and the artistic use of herbs.

Urban Herbs, Birmingham, West
Midlands

II

INTRODUCTION

The Knotte Garden Serveth for Pleasure:
The Potte Garden for Profitte.
                                    Horman, 1519

T HESE LINES from the second decade of the sixteenth century are a charming
   summation of herb gardens, for they should be both aesthetic and practical, the
herbs delightful to grow and useful for culinary, fragrant, medicinal and cosmetic
purposes.

There are few herb gardens in England – the Chelsea Physic Garden in London,
Oxburgh Hall in Norfolk and Broughton Hall in Yorkshire being exceptions – that
are older than the living model created by Vita Sackville-West and Harold Nicolson
at Sissinghurst Castle in Kent in 1937. Thus, almost all of the gardens in this book are
less than fifty years old. They mainly date from 1960 onwards, with many of them
being created during the 1970s when the general interest in herbs expanded
enormously, coinciding with people's desire or need to lead more healthy lives,
their growing aversion to packaged meals, increasing satisfaction from simpler,
well-flavoured foods, and wish to associate themselves when possible with pure and
natural products of all kinds.

Another most important contributing factor to the increased use of herbs,
beyond the Mint and Parsley ever present at the English Sunday lunch, was that
after the Second World War, travel to Europe became easier and consequently new-
found tastes such as Oregano and Basil from the Mediterranean countries could be
tried back home under the grey skies of England. Initially, the renewed knowledge
of herbs came from one sensuous and civilizing source – the splendid cookery books
by Elizabeth David. She has taught almost two generations about herbs in cookery
and much else besides. The dried herbs brought back from a holiday in France or
Italy were good and made food taste better. But, fresh-cut herbs are best and the
cultivation of herbs in pots, window boxes and gardens seems to be more and more a
delicious necessity, so that the broad renewal of interest in the growing of herbs has

Cosby House, Cosby, Leicestershire

become yet another manifestation of that uniquely English avocational obsession — the making and tending of gardens.

> They set great store by their gardens. In them they have vineyards, all manner of fruit, herbes and flowers, so pleasant, well-furnished and fynely kept. . . . Their studie and deligence herein cometh not only of pleasure, but also of a certain strife and contention that is betwene strete and strete, concerning the trimming, husbanding and furnishing of their gardens: every man for his owne parte.

Sir Thomas More's apt description from *Utopia*, written in 1519, still resonates with truth.

The photographs in this book illustrate a wide diversity in the design of herb gardens; some are rambling and informal, many more are contained and formal, but we have found a wonderful variety within both styles in situation, shape, planting and focal point. They can nestle safely within a church close in Lincolnshire, flourish in and revive a monastic cloister in Hampshire, embroider the vistas and immediate views from an Elizabethan country palace in Hertfordshire or from Carolean and Georgian manor houses grand or modest in Gloucestershire, Norfolk and Yorkshire, furnish a Yew-walled garden 'room' in Kent, humanize a cottage garden dominated by a nuclear power station's cooling towers, provide not only the display gardens but the stock plants for herb farms in Berkshire and Somerset, or be grown for educational purposes in Surrey.

There appears to be a strong collective historical consciousness about the basic design of herb gardens, which comes from the monastic tradition of growing herbs in a cloister bisected by paths with a well-head or some ornament in the centre. This quadrangle concept, though varied according to the size of the garden and through the individual imaginations of the many owners of the herb gardens seen here, still remains the major formal design mode. Very often the gardens are enclosed by walls or tall hedges, and Box shrub edging is used almost exclusively to define the beds of herb plants. Noteworthy examples of such strictly formal designs are at

Cranborne Manor, Wimborne, Dorset

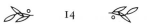

Young House at Wootton Rivers in Wiltshire and at Hardwick Hall in Derbyshire.

Informal herb gardens, which would appear superficially to offer much wider scope, seem generally too complicated a challenge, though there are most attractive ones at Denmans in West Sussex and Stoneacre in Kent. A possible reason for the paucity of new design ideas for herb gardens is that major garden designers have not been asked to tackle this question and if the making of new and more original herb gardens is to begin then such a design exercise is of paramount importance. There is an immense variety of herb material available most of which grows very easily in England and such a challenge would be exciting.

The purpose of the herb glossary in this book is two-fold. Firstly, the photographs can be helpful for identification and, secondly, some information on the history and cultivation is given for each herb. In addition, the photographer, Clive Boursnell, has devised a unique way of showing how beautiful herb plants are.

Herbs and certain cereals have been cultivated and used longer than any other type of plant. Artefacts from many cultures substantiate this – from Egyptian tomb paintings, Babylonian cuneiform tablets, Chinese bronzes of the Shang and Chou dynasties, Greek vases, stone stelae of the Mayans, frescoes at Pompeii, Khmer bas-reliefs at Angkor Wat, Persian and Mughal paintings, illuminated manuscripts from European monasteries to the earliest Italian Renaissance illustrated gardening books, which were the models for formal gardens in France and in Tudor, Jacobean and Carolean England. Herbs were planted in those English knot and parterre gardens of either geometric or sinuous embroidery shapes. They echoed the fashionable and fanciful patterns found in other decorative arts.

For thousands of years the primary application of herbs was medicinal. The deadly Aconite and Digitalis if used in small quantities have curative powers, while the gentle properties of Feverfew and Comfrey have been used in simple herbal remedies for centuries by country folk in England. The healing qualities of medicinal herbs were known in the infirmaries of monastic foundations and later this knowledge became the province of manor house still-rooms.

The benefit of certain pot or culinary herbs consumed in medieval times is still to be had in our kitchens today. Rosemary, Sage, Thyme and Fennel are four herbs with a long and venerable history in European cookery; records show that they were among the herb flavourings in Roman recipes. Bay, Lavender, Meadowsweet and Lad's Love are aromatic herbs that all have some fragrant and cosmetic values. The sixteenth-century French custom of using pleasant strewing herbs became popular in England during the time of Henry VIII. Branches of sweetly scented herbs were mixed with rushes and spread on the floors, which must have helped to make Tudor houses more attractive.

We searched out many more herb gardens than it is possible to include in this book, and no doubt many more exist, unknown to us, but it is very encouraging to have met so many people living in all parts of England who have decided to create these most traditional garden designs with pleasing enclaves of plants that uniquely combine the useful with the delightful.

Herb gardens – small, grand, modest, large, informal, formal – give to the owner, the designer, the gardener, the casual visitor sensations that we feel have been caught splendidly by Sir George Sitwell in his book *On the Making of Gardens*, published in 1909.

But whatever the garden is to be, whether its roses are to clamber up the eaves of a cottage or the towers of a palace, this at least is necessary, that it should be made with a care for the future and conviction of the importance of the task. According to Bacon, gardens are for refreshment; not for pleasure alone, nor even for happiness, but for the renewing rest that makes labour more fruitful, the unbending of a bow that it may shoot the stronger. In the ancient world it was ever the greatest of the emperors and the wisest of the philosophers that sought peace and rest in a garden.

BARNSLEY HOUSE

Barnsley, Gloucestershire

DAVID VEREY, the distinguished architectural historian who wrote the volumes on Gloucestershire and the Cotswolds for the Pevsner *Buildings of England* series, and his wife Rosemary Verey, the energetic, knowledgeable plantswoman, garden designer and writer on gardens, inherited Barnsley House more than thirty years ago, and after ten years occupation began to give serious consideration to the garden. Between them they have created one of the most famous gardens in England, reflecting their individual interests in the heritage of British architecture and garden design.

The house was built in 1697 and added to in 1830; the garden wall, and the Gothick summer house that is a pleasant termination of the wall, were built in 1770. In 1964 the Vereys added a Palladian Georgian summer house that was built in 1775 for the garden at nearby Fairford Park and moved to Barnsley. That year, a Laburnum walk was planted, which leads to a fountain by Simon Verity; the garden has other sculptures by him as well. In 1975, the narrow herb garden and the knot garden were laid out. For the last eight years, Rosemary Verey has been establishing a formal *jardin potager*, which has vegetable plots edged with herbs or Box radiating from a circular bed. There are Apple trees trained to goblet shapes and Bean-covered arbours for shelter from the sun or rain.

The knot garden is sited in front of the drawing room and is composed of two 12 ft (3.5 m) square lover's knots, edged with Box and made up of Golden Box, Wall Germander and *Phillyrea angustifolia*. The long herb bed placed near the kitchen door is 6 ft (1.8 m) by 45 ft (14 m) and patterned with a criss-cross of low Box hedges with 2 ft (60 cm) high Box pyramids to give vertical emphasis at either end. Each space between the criss-crossing is planted with a different herb, including all the common culinary herbs.

WESTBURY COURT

Westbury-on-Severn, Gloucestershire

THE GARDENS at Westbury Court include a superb water garden laid out in the seventeenth-century Dutch manner, one of the rare survivals of this type of garden in England. It is small in scale and contrasts with the large drawing and long vistas of the French formal garden. It was begun in 1696 by Maynard Colchester; the long canal was dug in that year, the hedges and topiary flanking it were planted in 1699, and the tall summer pavilion was built in 1702. A large house was built close to this garden in 1895, and the whole of it was almost lost when the house was demolished in 1960 and the property sold to a speculator. In 1967 the gardens were rescued and restored by The National Trust, helped enormously by the discovery of Colchester's account books dating from 1696 to 1705.

The interplay of water gardens, pavilion and sky produce a timeless picture, and as part of this fantasy the parterre has been restored at one side of the garden. Parterres were a seventeenth-century development from small early Renaissance knot gardens, and depend for their effect upon the symmetry of design. At Westbury Court there are two sets of matching 48 ft (14.6 m) square plots, each divided by two sets of paths crossing at right angles, and with a third bisecting the entire design, which is interrupted in the centre by a circular bed. All the beds are edged with dwarf Box and are defined by alternating topiary pyramids and balls of taller Box trees. They are filled with *Calendula officinalis*, *Echium creticum*, *Festuca ovina glauca*, *Iberis semperflorens* and *Salvia officinalis* 'Purpurascens', kept rigorously within the Box edging. This is using herb material at its most formal and in order for a parterre to be effective, great care must be taken over the choice of the plants and their mature heights. Formal parterre gardens must be maintained with a military precision and are the most labour intensive form of gardening, but their Apollonian effect is wonderfully satisfying.

ALDERLEY GRANGE

Alderley, Gloucestershire

THE CHANGE of ownership of a house often means that the garden changes its character. For many years, Alderley Grange belonged to Mr and Mrs James Lees-Milne and it was here that Avilde Lees-Milne created one of her most clever gardens, including a herb garden. In this happy instance the new owners, Mr Guy and The Hon. Mrs Acloque, have cherished and embellished this unique garden, meanwhile developing an attractive new garden of their own.

The herb garden is set in a corner where two high walls meet, and appears to the eye to be 30 ft (9 m) square. In fact, it is irregularly shaped, but one is deceived because the basic design is so strong. The design is of two superimposed crosses, similar to the pattern of the Union Jack, with an astrolabe in the centre. A hedge on the uneven side helps to make the total area seem square. All of the eight wedge-shaped beds are edged in Box, and the six furthest away from the entrance have neatly clipped standard Bay trees as foci. Each bed is planted with about ten different herbs ranging from Dwarf Comfrey to Golden Valerian. Spring bulbs and summer annuals are interplanted among the herbs.

Mr Acloque has recently established a new scented garden, 27 by 18 ft (8.2 by 5.5 m). In the centre is an Italian stone urn surrounded by a mass of Orris or Florentine Iris. Around this eight mop-headed, standard Privet trees are arranged in a square set on the diagonal. Other groupings of scented herbs include Green and Golden Sage, White Hyssop, *Santolina*, many old-fashioned *Dianthus*, and twenty-five different creeping Thymes. Many forms of scented *Pelargoniums* in pots are sunk into the garden during the summer and their leaves add a delightful marbled effect to this enchanting new corner at Alderley Grange.

STOKE LACY HERB FARM

Bromyard, Hereford and Worcester

Dᴜʀɪɴɢ the past century, the tradition of herbs and their uses has been kept alive by a number of English ladies, including Mrs C.W.Earle, with her book *Pot-Pourri from a Surrey Garden*, Miss Eleanour Sinclair Rohde, Miss Gertrude Jekyll, Vita Sackville-West and Miss Margaret Brownlow at the legendary herb farm and garden at Seal in Kent, where so many ladies trained who have since grown herbs, both professionally and for their own pleasure. Mrs Madge Hooper at Stoke Lacy belongs to this tradition and maintains one of England's oldest established herb farms. She was selling a very wide range of unusual herbs when they were virtually unobtainable elsewhere in this country, and she evangelized herbs by lecturing to anyone who would listen both here and abroad. Today, she tries to limit her activities somewhat and though the business of the farm is reduced, she laid out a new display garden there in 1984.

This garden is 30 ft (9 m) square with four curving beds divided by paths and centred on a shell-shaped garden ornament. Mrs Hooper's knowledge, gathered over so many years, has culminated in this garden, which contains about 180 different herbs. Its attraction lies in the skill with which one herb is juxtaposed with another in order to emphasize their individual characteristics, and very different shapes and colours. Low-growing herbs are graded against taller ones, dark green against pale green, feathery-leaved against dense-leaved. Such a garden may appear to the visitor to be very casual and simple, but such an apparently uncontrived design only results from the experience gained by many years of hard work, attention to detail and a compulsive love of herbs and their characteristics, all of which are exemplified in Madge Hooper's latest garden.

MAWLEY HALL

Cleabury Mortimer, Shropshire

MAWLEY HALL is one of the finest examples of the grand Baroque, early Georgian brick houses that are to be found in the west midlands. The front is ornamented with two-storey pilasters and it commands extensive views of the Shropshire countryside from the eminence on which it is built. The ground immediately around the house is landscaped in the traditional English style of spreading lawns, mature trees and strategically placed statues, urns and columned temple. The garden renaissance at Mawley Hall is due to the interest and care of Mr and Mrs Anthony Galliers-Pratt. Mrs Galliers-Pratt is the enthusiastic gardener of the family and she has been responsible for planning the herb garden. It connects the formal garden with the swimming pool, which is sited in front of a Georgian stable-block, now converted into a house. The transition from the grand to the domestic has been well handled, and a background suited both to the casualness of the swimming pool and to the grandness of the created landscape has been sympathetically designed.

The herb garden exists in an area 75 by 50 ft (23 by 15 m). There is a wide path leading from the main gardens to the pool bordered on both sides by five matching columnar Junipers and framed with Box. On either side of the Junipers are three long interlocking rectangular beds filled with about 200 different varieties of herbs, and bordered by low brick walls supporting wide brick paths. One of the brick paths has many varieties of creeping Thymes, *Thymus serpyllum, Camomile treneague* and Penny-royal planted in between the bricks, which give up their various scents when crushed underfoot. Beyond this on a raised bank is a procession of six life-sized statues, mirrored on the opposite side by five more columnar Junipers. Near the stable end of the garden shrubs and Magnolias have been planted, which are reflected in the black mirror surface of the swimming pool.

OAK COTTAGE HERB FARM

Nesscliffe, Shropshire

THERE must be something about the air around the village of Little Ness, as there are now three herb farms within five miles of that village. Mrs Ruth Thompson has lived in Oak Cottage for some years and has established a very well-known herb farm where she grows and sells more than 400 different varieties of herbs. At one time she cultivated fields of Thyme for drying, but asthma forced her to abandon that project. Yet her enthusiasm for herbs remains unabated, and in the space behind her house she has created the dream cottage garden. The area is 120 by 75 ft (36.5 by 23 m), bisected by paths and towards the centre a low rectangular Yew hedge. In the corner furthest from the cottage is a summer house with a pond, and at the other side an area in which container-grown herbs are kept.

The rest of the garden is filled with a mixture of old-fashioned cottage plants and herbs. There is no formal arrangement but each plant is chosen for its decorative qualities. The planting is changed each year, inspired by new ideas for combinations of herbs or the need to include another rare herb plant. Most of us have a vision of what a typical cottage garden looks like, a style that has become increasingly rare as horticultural fashions change and the available plant material is standardized. It requires much expertise to create the desired effect of masses of different flowers mostly in bloom interspersed with well-established and useful herbs, typical of a good cottage garden. It is also labour intensive, but Mrs Thompson's dogged perserverance is well rewarded when visitors to Oak Cottage see her garden in its glory during the summer months.

MALLORY COURT

Leamington Spa, Warwickshire

As 'foodie' journalists tell us every Sunday about the more *raffinés* aspects of cookery, and extoll the brilliance of country house hotels and their kitchens, we would expect herb gardens to be an integral part of all such establishments. Yet the only hotel we have found so far to have a herb garden of any serious extent is Mallory Court. The house was built in 1915 in the grand neo-Georgian, Cotswold style. Jeremy Mort and Allan Holland bought it in 1974, and have since restored the gardens to their original grandeur. The care they have lavished on the hotel means that it is one of the few British members of the most prestigious *Relais de Campagne — Relais Gourmets — Grands Hôtels*.

Four years ago, in the old vegetable garden, they laid out a very large herb garden that was mainly to serve the kitchens, but was also intended as an attraction for their guests. The garden is 120 by 45 ft (36.5 by 14 m) with a wide central path, in the middle of which is a circular bed with a Bay tree. Ten beds are placed on either side, rectangular shaped in the middle and triangular shaped at either end. All the beds are edged with Cotton Lavender or Wall Germander and are planted with about fifty different herbs. Big commercial kitchens need quantities of Parsley, Chives, Marjoram, Chervil, Mint, Sage and, particularly, French Tarragon. There are two sorts of Tarragon, the French type, *Artemisia dracunculus*, and the Russian form, which is *Artemisia dracunculoides*. The latter can be raised from seed, grows to about 4 ft (1.2 m) and is best used to screen dustbins or the compost heap. The true French Tarragon has a unique Anise taste. It is usually only increased by root propagation, reaches a height of 18 in (45 cm) and needs to be somewhat protected in the winter. Mallory Court of course has the correct type and the garden is a delight to behold when in flower for it presents a marvellous evocation of the perfect herb garden.

LEA FORD COTTAGE

Adams Hill Power Station, Sutton Coldfield, West Midlands

Herb gardens can be found in the most unexpected places. When we were carrying out the initial research for this book, somebody mentioned that they had heard of a herb garden in the grounds of a power station. The site was easy to find because of the four immense cooling towers that dominate the landscape of West Birmingham, which stand on part of a 1,000 acre estate owned by The Central Electricity Generating Board. A section of the estate is used for recreational activities by the employees of the CEGB and another part as an area for environmental studies. One of the buildings is a seventeenth-century farm worker's home, now called Lea Ford Cottage; in 1675 it was known as Maggotts Crofte. The cottage, which is wood-framed wattle and daub with unglazed mullion windows, has been reconstructed using traditional building methods, and school children can now see what housing was really like for most people in seventeenth-century England – two up, two down and very draughty.

A herb garden has been planted in front of the cottage in an area 21 by 15 ft (6.4 by 4.5 m). There is a Strawberry patch and beyond that an area irregularly planted with ten different herbs; a lot of Marjoram, some Sage and Thyme, and, in order to give a visual focus, a large clump of Cardoons, *Scolymus cardunculus*, in one corner. This is a member of the Artichoke family; Dioscorides refers to its cultivation on a large scale near Great Carthage and Pliny wrote of its medicinal virtues. The young blanched stems are delicious to eat. It also makes a good yellow dye and it is used as a substitute for rennet in the making of cheeses. Finding this plant in the herb garden in front of Lea Ford Cottage was almost as surprising as finding the seventeenth-century cottage next to a twentieth-century power station.

URBAN HERBS
Birmingham, West Midlands

Paul Stocking must have the most unlikely location in England for a herb farm. It is in the back garden of a terrace house in central Birmingham, an area that is in need of urban renewal. Across the road is the local 'self-sufficiency' garden with two goats that will eat anything they are allowed, and more; they also act as a most unusual early warning system. Stocking has made a garden 40 by 14 ft (12 by 4.2 m), with eight beds retained by 7 in (18 cm) high board surrounds, and with two terracotta pots as focal points to the plan. In these beds, and in two long borders on either side, grow 140 different types of herbs.

The beds are planted by botanical family: from the *Rosaceae* there is the Apothecary's Rose and Meadowsweet; from *Boraginaceae*, Lungwort and Borage; from *Leguminosae*, Melilot and Woad; and from *Scrophulariaceae*, Mullein and Figwort. There are two beds for the *Labiatae* family from which come many culinary herbs, including Thyme, Sage, Hyssop, Lemon Balm and Rosemary. Then there are two beds of *Compositae*, which include Tansy, Curry Plant, the Cotton Lavenders and the Artemisias such as Southernwood or Lad's Love and Mugwort. Between the house and the display garden are the two wide borders containing plants from the *Liliaceae*, *Umbelliferae* and *Ranunculaceae* families and the *Mentha* genus, of which about twenty different specimens are planted here. Rarely have we seen a small garden that contains such a wide collection of herb material. Most of the species are available for sale to those who visit Urban Herbs, and who are intrigued enough by what they see to wish to make herb gardens of their own in similar restricted circumstances.

MOSELEY OLD HALL

Wolverhampton, West Midlands

Moseley Old Hall is an Elizabethan house, initially half-timbered and now brick-faced, which lies between a motorway and the outskirts of Wolverhampton. It was here that King Charles II sheltered after the Battle of Worcester, and it has the bed in which he slept and the 'hide' in which he was concealed from Cromwell's army. It now belongs to The National Trust, who have reconstructed a formal knot garden on the west side of the house, based on the original 1640 design of a Reverend Walter Stonehouse. It includes a wooden arbour from a pattern in *The Gardener's Labyrinth* by William Hill, 1577. The garden was re-planned with the help of Graham Stuart Thomas and Alice Coats who also helped with the selection of herbaceous plants in other parts of the garden.

The stunningly simple formal garden has a long Hornbeam arbour on one side, and the entire area is divided into eleven repeating patterns. There is a circular bed in the middle of each section with a formally clipped, standard Bay tree in each as a vertical focal point. All the beds are edged with Box. The circular beds are in-filled with large grey pebbles around the Bay trees, and two different coloured gravels are used as backgrounds for the other beds. The Bays and the Box hedging are meticulously trimmed so that when the garden is viewed from an upper room the design becomes a wonderful carpet composed solely of plant and gravel elements. Such a garden is necessarily time consuming, and in the restricted area of the gardens at Moseley Old Hall we see laid out before us a marvellously accurate historical foil to the ancient house.

COSBY HOUSE

Cosby, Leicestershire

COSBY HOUSE is seventeenth century with some Georgian alterations, but the property also includes a fine sixteenth-century timber-frame barn with brick in-filling, which dates from 1766, and later stabling ranged around a cobbled yard. The herb garden is the central incident of the large main garden, from which the owner, Mrs Jane Faire, sells herbs and organizes courses on herb gardening.

The design of the herb garden is a six-pointed star formed by two interlocking equilateral triangles set within a circle; the garden is 20 ft (6 m) square. The plan was taken from *The New Orchard and Garden*, written by William Lawson in 1618, a year after he had completed *The Countrie Housewife's Garden*, the first book on gardening for women. Mrs Faire considers the design simple enough to be plotted by any unmathematical gardener. The star is delineated with Box and Santolina, and at its centre is a small statue. Lavender encircles the design, with Pinks used as points of colour.

THE IZAAK WALTON COTTAGE
Shugborough, Staffordshire

Izaak Walton is known to all as the author of *The Compleat Angler*. Born in 1593, he died in 1683 at the age of 90, greatly respected as a fine biographer who was much concerned with the religious controversies of the seventeenth century. His first work was *An Elegy on Dr Donne*; the poet and divine was one of Walton's greatest friends. *The Compleat Angler* was a product of his leisure and re-popularized in 1750 after Dr Samuel Johnson had written about it. Walton spent part of his life in Staffordshire, where he owned a property called Halfhead Farm, which he made over as a legacy to Stafford Corporation and which was finally bought by the Izaak Walton Cottage Trust in 1923. Though he would have known the cottage, it was never his permanent home and contains no objects intimately associated with him. It is, however, a typical seventeenth-century cottage and the interior has been furnished with objects from that period.

The herb garden is 50 by 35 ft (15 by 10.6 m), and is divided into two small and two large beds surrounded by a path bordered by Yew hedges. The herbs chosen are mainly those that would have been used in the late seventeenth century. At that time the emphasis was on herbs for medicinal purposes and on those that made a house smell more sweetly; until a hundred years ago, herbal remedies were used by most families. The herb garden at Izaak Walton Cottage reminds us how recently it was that we all depended on such plants to make our lives more healthy and tolerable.

HOLME PIERREPONT HALL

Nottingham, Nottinghamshire

Holme Pierrepont Hall is a remarkable example of an early Tudor manor house. It contains medieval lodgings, one with a superb timbered ceiling dating from the 1400s, and the Big Room has been restored as a venue for operas and concerts. The Pierrepont family lived here for centuries.

The Victorian garden in the internal courtyard was laid out in 1875. At the same time the arcades were erected on two sides, designed by the agent, a Mr Beaumont, and the vicar, a Mr Seymour. The garden, approximately 90 by 33 ft (27.5 by 10 m), is an elaborate example of its period, with a sundial in the centre balanced by two circular beds and criss-crossed with paths separating small beds, which combine to form an elaborate parterre design. There are few such complete Victorian gardens left, and the original plan was shown in 1979 in *The Garden* exhibition at The Victoria and Albert Museum, which coincidentally celebrated the centennial of the coming of age of the then heir to Holme Pierrepont, Viscount Newark, subsequently the fourth Earl Manvers.

In Victorian times such a scheme would not have been planted solely with herbs, but would have also included bedding-out plants, arranged formally and changed with the seasons. The present owners, Mr and Mrs R.Brackenbury, follow this tradition and plant the herbs that grow most successfully in these conditions, intermingling them with annual and perennial flowers that are suitable to the period of the garden. It is an evocative re-creation of a type of garden planting that has gone almost completely out of fashion, but might originally have intrigued 'Maud' to 'come into the garden'.

HARDWICK HALL

Chesterfield, Derbyshire

Hardwick Hall was the culmination of the construction mania of Elizabeth Cavendish, fifth Countess of Shrewsbury. Known as 'building Bess Hardwick', she outlived four husbands, each one richer than the last, and finally built for herself in the last years of the sixteenth century a fantastical country palace in the Derbyshire Fells of northern England. Contemporary grandees called it 'Hardwick Hall, more glass than wall'. For 350 years it slumbered as the Dower House for the Duchesses of Devonshire, but in 1950 it was given slightly unwillingly and in lieu of death duties to The National Trust, which now cares for the house and the grounds and has added a magnificent herb garden to parallel the extraordinary Hall.

The herb garden occupies one-quarter of the enormous walled garden. It is 200 by 100 ft (61 by 30.5 m) and divided by two *allées*, one of Yew and one of Hornbeam. Each main section is a rectangle surrounded by two very wide borders. Trees are planted in each corner and the geometric design is further enhanced by pyramids of either variegated Hops or Beans, grown on tall stakes. Some of the beds are edged with the shiny-leaved Wall Germander. The individual beds are so large that were the hundred different herb species they contain not planted in enormous drifts they would seem quite insignificant. This is a herb garden in which the boldest pallette of plant material was needed and here it has been used admirably in both form and scale. It is slightly ironic that such a very English garden should have been tended and nurtured for its first eight or nine years by a Polish refugee, Mr John Jennings, who is now head gardener at the Prime Minister's country residence, Chequers.

LITTLE MORETON HALL

Congleton, Cheshire

Lɪᴛᴛʟᴇ Mᴏʀᴇᴛᴏɴ Hᴀʟʟ is possibly the most perfect example of a moated black-and-white, half-timbered manor house in England. The house was finally completed by the Moreton family in the sixteenth century, and illustrates a merging of the closed medieval Gothic style with the open exuberance of the English Renaissance in domestic architecture. The house is surrounded by a moat, beyond which on one side is planted a formal Elizabethan knot garden. The area is 60 ft (18 m) square and is based on a design from Leonard Meager's *The Complete Gardener*, published in 1670. It was re-planned in 1975 by Paul Mills.

The garden is entirely bounded by a new Yew hedge and is divided into four equal sections with wide, shallow, scalloped inner edges, bordered on two sides by formally planted rectangular beds. All the beds are outlined by low clipped Yew and the design is further emphasized by gravel. Fifty different herb species are arranged symmetrically so that the design looks like a living embroidery. It is a complicated design that echoes the robustness of the half-timbered patterns that are such a spectacular part of the fabric of Little Moreton Hall. The National Trust has an enormous number of gardens to care for, and it is encouraging to see how it takes this responsibility seriously and creates new gardens that perfectly reflect the houses in its care.

LEDSHAM HERB GARDEN

The University of Liverpool Botanic Gardens, Ness, Cheshire

Ness Gardens were laid out by the late Arthur Bulley in 1898, when he built a house with commanding views over the Dee Estuary and the Welsh hills. He was an enthusiastic plant collector and created gardens covering some 62 acres. In 1948 his daughter gave the whole estate to the University of Liverpool to be kept as a botanic garden with specified areas for public access.

A recent development is the Ledsham Herb Garden, planted in 1974. This is a long rectangular garden with the subsidiary beds divided by two major paths, one covered with an arched Laburnum tunnel that blooms in early summer.

There are twenty-four beds, each containing either one or two types of herb, planted according to their varying heights. Amongst the herbs are Summer Savory, Greater Burnet, Tree Onion, Angelica and *Rheum palmatum*. The Mints are carefully separated into smaller beds so that their spreading invasive habit can be contained. A bed of Basil is also planted out in the late spring after the frosts have gone, so that visitors can appreciate this delicious aromatic herb, which grows so vigorously in Mediterranean countries, but which needs great care if it is to be grown successfully in England, where it rarely gets sufficient sun or the watering it needs at midday. Off the main herb garden is an *allée* of Lime trees, behind which are railings with Braille labels so that the blind may identify highly scented plants such as *Daphne odora*, Lemon Verbena, Pineapple Sage, Heliotrope, the evergreen Honeysuckle and *Rhododendron fragrantissimum*, among many others.

ABBEY HOUSE MUSEUM

Leeds, West Yorkshire

M ANY PEOPLE only think of Leeds as being one of the great centres of nineteenth-century commerce, as it is closely associated with the heavy industry that once produced so much wealth for England. The centre of the town has some very grand Victorian buildings, but its economic connections with the wool trade go back many more centuries to medieval times. Two miles from the city centre are the ruins of an old abbey church and on gently sloping ground across the road is the Abbey House Museum.

This is enclosed by a small park, in the centre of which is a herb garden, 75 by 50 ft (23 by 15 m), designed in 1960 as a memorial to a former Lord Mayor of Leeds, Mrs Mary Pierce. The design is fairly conventional with a medieval stone stump in the centre and two rectangular beds on either side, each surrounded by four interlocking beds. Steps lead to York stone paths and the garden is bordered by a wide Lavender hedge.

About thirty different species are to be found in this garden, with a particular emphasis on many varieties of *Thymus*. These plants thrive in a very sunny well-drained position and Wild Thyme, mentioned by Shakespeare, grows superbly on this site. Generally, if you want to use herbs for culinary purposes they should not be allowed to flower as this dissipates their essential oils, but the mats and cushions of Thyme in flower in this garden add greatly to its attraction. The local people obviously find the garden very restful in spite of the adjacent main road, and we hope that while sitting there, they might think of the abbey gardens now long gone that would have contained many of the herbs enjoyed here today.

YORK GATE

Leeds, West Yorkshire

MRS SYBIL SPENCER showed no surprise at all when we called to visit her herb garden. She correctly expected there to be recognition after the long years that she has spent making a beautiful garden in one acre in a pleasant suburb of Leeds. The garden demonstrates both her knowledge of horticulture and her very considerable talents as a garden designer. The area is divided into separate sections, one with water, another influenced by Japanese gardens, a Nut walk, a Peony bed, an Iris border, a white and silver garden, a pavement or foot maze and a miniature Pinetum.

The herb garden, enclosed on two sides by a tall Yew hedge, is 30 by 10 ft (9 by 3 m). There is a wide central path leading to a pillared summer house at the end. Four variegated Box-tree globes signal the changing shape of the path and four corkscrew Box trees are placed at either end of the two main herb borders. Fifty different herbs are grown, including Red Sage, Giant Alliums, Bronze Fennel, Angelica and Golden Balm. Great care has been taken in chosing herb plants for their contrasting colours, and the garden is a most pleasant design created with dark and pale greens, gold, bronze and yellow, sparkling with the occasional white or pink star-like flowers of many different herbs. This is a garden for contemplation; the formal summer house is a perfect place to sit and allow one's thoughts to become calm and enjoy the garden's beauty.

STOCKELD PARK

Wetherby, North Yorkshire

S TOCKELD PARK, designed by James Paine in 1758, is a magnificent estate in the Vale of York. The house has splendid interiors with a fine Crinoline staircase and is lived in by Mrs Rosalind Gough, whose family bought the estate in the nineteenth century. It is surrounded by a wide park, and immediately to the south of the house is a small herb garden.

This garden was designed by John Codrington who also designed the herb garden in the Kitchen Court at Emmanuel College, Cambridge. The area chosen is 30 ft (9 m) square and contains four large circular beds 10 ft (3 m) in diameter, with four smaller circular beds laid out in a regular pattern in the centre. The shape of the beds is formed from concrete, and the largest have dividers so that they resemble cartwheels. The herbs are planted in a weed-suppressing ground cover of gravel, which provides a background to the different leaf textures. The neat dark green *Cupressus fastigiatus* 'Skyrocket' gives vertical focus.

It is often recommended in books on herb garden design that a cartwheel be used as a suitable layout for growing herbs. However, a great deal of care must be taken in the choice of the plants for an awareness of the full height of each herb is essential if the design is to be effective. If large herbs such as Angelica, Lovage, or Chervil are used, the planting will look very unbalanced in high summer; it is also essential that the herbs be trimmed so that the basic design is always evident and not overwhelmed by the taller plants. The gardens at Stockeld are well maintained and demonstrate how effective such designs can be when laid out by an expert.

HARLOW CAR GARDENS
Harrogate, North Yorkshire

HARLOW CAR is the headquarters of The Northern Horticultural Society, which funds eleven specialist plant groups: Alpine and Rock Plants; Delphiniums; Edible Plants; Garden Science; Heathers; Lilies; Rhododendrons; Roses; Trees, Shrubs and Hardy Plants; Orchids and Ferns, though none specifically relates to herbs. However, the herbs grown in these gardens could persuade members or anyone who lives in a cool climate, to become enthusiastic about them. The herb garden, 90 by 42 ft (27.5 by 12.8 m), is south-facing and surrounded by high stone walls. Long stone paths divide the area into three sections, and the borders next to the walls have intersecting paths at 15 ft (4.5 m) intervals so that the herbs grown there can be studied conveniently and tended easily. When planning a new herb garden it is best not to have beds more than 6 ft (1.8 m) wide as this basic dimension makes the planting, weeding and harvesting of the herbs so much easier.

Even though this garden is in the north of England it grows a selection of herbs that could be found much further south. The beds by the walls are filled mainly with ground-cover herbs such as creeping Thymes, Periwinkles and Bugles. A couple of beds are planted with Heathers, and in the long central bed, sixty different herbs are grown where the sunny aspect and the protecting walls ensure that they come to a fine maturity. Most perennial herbs are very hardy and as long as the soil is well drained they should flourish throughout England and in similar temperate regions with few problems. The herb garden at Harlow Car is proof of this.

BROUGHTON HALL

Skipton, North Yorkshire

Twenty-nine generations of the Tempest family have lived at Broughton Hall since 1120, which is unique in the history of the handful of proud and stubborn Roman Catholic families who kept their faith alive in England during the Reformation. It was not until the latter half of the eighteenth century that the family had accumulated sufficient money to renovate the old manor and in 1810 two wings and the imposing Ionic portico were added. The interior was also refurbished at that time and much of the furniture that is still in the house was made by the London-based firm, Waring and Gillow.

At the sides of the house, landscaped lawns rise steeply to a wooded skyline. The beautiful conservatory, built on the basilica plan, the terraces and the Italian garden with its balustrades and statues, were all the work of William Nesfield, an army officer turned landscape gardener who was the friend of the celebrated painter, J. M. W. Turner. Nesfield wrote to Sir Charles Tempest, 'You have certainly given me the most difficult job that I have ever experienced.' His garden here is a triumph over nature's unaccommodating terrain. To the west of the house on a steep slope he planned two elaborate parterres in the French style. The first is a rectangle, 90 by 60 ft (27.5 by 18 m), adjacent to which is a second parterre, 30 by 20 ft (9 by 6 m), with irregularly curving sides. The designs of both are delineated by sturdy low Box hedging with gravel paths in between. Both parterres are meticulously trimmed and it is very encouraging to find such established examples of high-Victorian gardening, since most parterres from that era have long since disappeared.

ACORN BANK
Penrith, Cumbria

THE NATIONAL TRUST has many unknown gems among its possessions and one of them is the herb garden at Acorn Bank. The long, pink granite, sixteenth-century mansion is now a Sue Ryder Home, but in an old walled garden beyond the house The Trust has created one of the most interesting medicinal herb gardens in England. Some years ago they had an appeal for £30,000 to fund this garden, which is looked after by only one gardener and the regional information officer on a part-time basis.

Between the eleventh and sixteenth centuries, Acorn Bank belonged to The Knights Templars and The Knights Hospitallers and thus it seemed particularly suitable to concentrate on medicinal herbs in this garden. The garden is protected by a low sandstone wall and Damson trees to the south. The north wall is 9 ft (2.7 m) high, made of brick, was at one time heated, and is at least 250 years old. There is a tall Holly hedge at one end and a small greenhouse at the other.

The herb garden was laid out in 1962. The two long beds are divided by two wide paths; in the middle of the central bed is a Quince tree. The garden is 45 by 22 ft (13.7 by 6.7 m) and there is a Peony border by the entrance. Among the medicinal plants are Cranesbill, Danewort, Redspur Valerian, Belladonna, Thornapple, Pokeweed, Horehound, Wood Sanicle, Betony, Yellow Flag, Feverfew, Viper's Bugloss, Fleabane, Double Crow's Foot, American Spikenard, Arnica, Henbane, Opium Poppy, Pasque Flower, Hemlock, Comfrey, Asarabacca, Selfheal, Birthroot, Bloodroot, Monkshood, Foxglove, Lily-of-the-Valley and the Royal Fern. It is an amazing collection of plants and on a summer day this garden, redolent with many scents, is an inspiration to all those who realise how important medicinal herbs have been to mankind, and how beautiful they can be when grown in a sympathetic setting.

PETERBOROUGH CATHEDRAL
Peterborough, Cambridgeshire

M RS ELIZABETH PEPLOW has recently designed the herb garden at Peterborough Cathedral. In the course of the research she did before planning the garden, she found that in 1302 the Abbot 'Had made a beautiful herber next to the Derby yard — *Gardiaum Dereby* — and surrounded it with double moats, with bridges and lovely plants — *Herbies delicatissimis*'. The area of that particular 'herber' was two acres and cost £25, which is the equivalent of £15,000 today. We know where its site was from a plan in John Harvey's book, *Medieval Gardens*, 1981, but the new herb garden is placed against the south-facing cloister wall. It is 120 by 3 ft (36.5 m by 90 cm), and Mrs Peplow has restricted her choice of plants to those that would have been found in the original 'herber', including Angelica, Bay, Camomile, Wall Germander, Golden Marjoram, Golden Thyme, Hyssop, Lady's Mantle, Lavender, Lily, *Lilium candidum*, Myrtle, Peony, Pennyroyal, Pomegranate, Rose, Rosemary, Rue, Sage, Southernwood, Tansy, Thyme and Sweet Woodruff.

It is particularly appropriate that Pomegranate was planted, since the fruit was the emblem of Catherine of Aragon, King Henry VIII's first wife, who is buried in the cathedral precinct. His divorce from Catherine led to the Dissolution of the Monasteries; the monastery at Peterborough was dissolved in 1539, but was re-dedicated as a cathedral in 1541. Mrs Peplow's careful reconstruction gives an accurate idea of the plants that the monks of this foundation would have used, and the garden is a tribute to her scholarship.

EMMANUEL COLLEGE
Cambridge, Cambridgeshire

EMMANUEL COLLEGE is unique among Oxford and Cambridge colleges in having a herb garden in its Kitchen Court. Good food has been a preoccupation over many centuries of those dining at High Table, though such interest rarely extended to the food prepared for the undergraduates. In 1961, Emmanuel College decided to re-plan its Kitchen Court and asked John Codrington to prepare designs. He noted that the Court is not a regular rectangle and that undergraduates cross the court by several different routes depending upon which door or entrance is their objective. The spaces left between such naturally emergent paths have become the shapes of the beds that are now filled with herbs. This means that the overall design has a rather angular geometry and is modernistic in feeling – a frisson from the time of the Festival of Britain (1951). The beds are edged with Box and planted with about twenty different herb species.

Codrington originally suggested that these be grown through different gravels and that anthracite coal chips be used for the ground cover to emphasize the foliage of variegated Mint and Golden Feverfew. Different coloured gravels were widely used in the sixteenth and seventeenth centuries to highlight the elaborate designs of knot gardens. Sometimes chips of glass were added so the gardens would glitter in the sun.

Codrington planted a Bay tree in the centre of one bed and a Eucalyptus in the middle of another, but failed to warn the gardeners that they should be kept at a similar height, so the Bay is now dwarfed by the Eucalyptus, which is some 30 ft (9 m). However, the simple strength of this herb garden design is such that it looks very attractive in the winter and under snow it reminds one of a Japanese woodcut.

OXBURGH HALL

Swaffham, Norfolk

OXBURGH HALL was built in 1482 by Sir Edmund Bendingfeld, and has remained in the family for over 450 years, being given to The National Trust by The Dowager Lady Bendingfeld in 1952. Of mellow red brick, surrounded by a wide moat and with a magnificent gate tower the house is one of the most romantic of its period to have survived.

The roof of the tower gives a splendid view of the gardens, particularly of the French formal garden, a magnificent eighteenth-century-style parterre almost identical to the one illustrated in *La Théorie et la Pratique du Jardinage* by Antoine Joseph Dezallier D'Argenville, 1709. This design was used in a garden near Paris where members of the Bendingfeld family saw it in about 1845. Gravel is used as the background and contrast to the planting, and to make the paths within the composition. From a central circular bed four large scrolls radiate enclosing two stylized palmate-shaped beds, with formalized *fleur des lys* at top and bottom. Sixteen Box-tree balls punctuate the design, which is outlined by Box-edged beds divided by the gravel. The main shapes are formed by trimmed *Santolina chamaecyparissus* and *Ruta graveolens* 'Jackman's Blue', interplanted with *Tagetes patula* and *Ageratum houstonianum*. The parterre was restored some years ago from a semi-derelict condition by The National Trust, who sensibly replaced most of the annual bedding plants with permanent perennial planting.

Beyond this parterre is another garden enclosed by a Yew hedge and tall brick walls. In one corner is a triangular bed 18 ft (5.5 m) at its widest point and 72 ft (22 m) long, this is filled with forty different culinary herbs that might have been used in the kitchens of Oxburgh Hall when the original builder, Sir Edmund, entertained King Richard III.

NETHERFIELD HERBS

Rougham, Suffolk

I N 1977, we had our initiation into preparing a herb display for The Chelsea Flower Show. In the same year Lesley Bremness won the *Garden News* competition to design a herb garden for The Herb Society. She was sufficiently encouraged by this success to start her own herb farm and to lay out a display herb garden beside her sixteenth-century cottage. Nether Street is a road connecting fields rather than houses and here she has planned a rectangular garden 45 by 33 ft (14 by 10 m) in the middle of the lawn. The central bed is laid out on a diagonal and crossed by brick paths. The entrance has a 'welcome mat' of lawn Camomile and at the opposite end is a Camomile-turfed seat, which was first mentioned as a garden conceit by Sir Francis Bacon in his famous essay *On Gardens*, 1625.

On either side of the Camomile mat are two smaller knot borders, and they are balanced at the other end by two beds, one containing medicinal herbs and the other salad herbs of the sixteenth century. These complement the period of the cottage. The centre beds contain four groups of herbs, six different Sages, six Marjorams, six Rosemarys and twenty-five creeping Thymes. On one side there is a long border containing tall herbs with a seat in the middle protected by an arbour covered with Purple Grape, Honeysuckle, Jasmine, Roses and *Akebia quinata*. On the other side, beyond the herb garden proper, is a Cherry walk carpeted with bulbs in the spring. Lesley Bremness has found room for more than 200 herbs in her herb garden, and she offers for sale a range of some 150 different types. She also salutes her nationality by growing many herbs from Canadian seeds, which she is sent from time to time.

GAINSBOROUGH'S HOUSE

Sudbury, Suffolk

GAINSBOROUGH'S HOUSE is a typical eighteenth-century town house built in brick with a central portico. Thomas Gainsborough, the most famous of the eighteenth-century portrait painters, was born here in 1727. The house is now the headquarters of The Gainsborough's House Society and contains many reference documents and drawings associated with the artist. A herb garden has been laid out at the back of the house in the old town garden.

The garden is 70 by 27 ft (21 by 8.2 m), with a wide path leading from the back door to a high wall at the end. A border of Lavender is placed on one side of the path with bushes of Rosemary and golden Irish Yews planted near the door; two square beds are separated from rectangular borders by paving stones and there is a black Mulberry tree that was 120 years old at the time of Gainsborough's birth. A very simple planting plan has been adopted using fifteen different herbs, which make an effective display and a garden that is easy to maintain. Perennial herbs need very little attention once they are established, so long as the aspect is reasonably sunny and the soil well drained. They merely need to be cut back in the autumn and the beds tidied up in the spring before new growth begins. They rarely require feeding, since fertilizer produces rampant foliage thus decreasing the pungency of the essential oils.

KNEBWORTH HOUSE

Knebworth, Hertfordshire

KNEBWORTH has been the home of the Lytton family since 1492. The present early Victorian high Gothick confection, erected *c.*1830, is one-quarter of the original house and was redesigned by Sir Edward Bulwer Lytton and his mother Lady Elizabeth in an effort to recreate both externally and internally what they fondly imagined to be a realistic medieval mansion. His daughter, Lady Emily, married the Edwardian architect Sir Edwin Lutyens, and it was he who was responsible for replanning the gardens in 1908 with the help of his mentor and collaborator, Miss Gertrude Jekyll. The rectangle of pleached Lime trees around the pool outside the garden front has a Mughal feeling to recall the viceroyalty of India of the then Lord Lytton. The house passed through the female line to the current occupiers, The Honourable David and Mrs Lytton-Cobbold, who today maintain their gardens with only three gardeners, instead of the fourteen that were employed before the First World War.

Gertrude Jekyll designed the planting plan for five circular, interlocking brick beds called a *quincunx*. However, the planting was never carried out. In 1980, the Landscape Department of the University of California at Berkeley informed the family that Miss Jekyll's original plan was held in their archives. Two years later, using this plan, the *quincunx* was reconstructed in brick and planted with the herbs that she had originally specified: Southernwood, Tarragon, Alecost, Hyssop, Balm, Rue, Common Thyme, Rosemary, Sage, Lavender, Cotton Lavender, Chervil, Summer and Winter Savory, Fennel, Marjoram and Horehound. It is particularly felicitous that a small herb garden by two of England's greatest designers now enriches an ancient house so redolent of history and romance.

HATFIELD HOUSE
Hatfield, Hertfordshire

WHEN Lord and Lady Salisbury inherited Hatfield House in 1972, they found the great Jacobean palace was well preserved, but the encompassing gardens dull; all traces of the gardens designed in 1609 by John Tradescant the Elder for Sir Robert Cecil had inevitably long since disappeared.

Today, there are four beautiful gardens. The first is a formal garden below the wide terrace on the east front of the house. A stone balustraded double staircase leads down to this garden, which is bordered on two sides by *allées* of standard clipped Ilex. In the centre are eight square beds edged with Box and filled with old-fashioned Roses, flowering shrubs and herbs, which are encouraged to grow to their full size. The second garden is below the west front and is a large rectangular plot contained on two sides by Lime arbours. Within tall Yew hedges are enclosed four large beds filled with scented plants and bordered with Lavender; in the centre is a fountain to beguile the visitor with the sound from its water jet. Below this is the third garden, which is a herb garden set in the middle of a lawn. The garden is rectangular, divided by Camomile paths, with three concentric oval beds centred on a sundial. These are planted with all the common culinary herbs, and with Honeysuckle standards used as vertical focal points.

The fourth garden, in front of the remaining wing of the Old Palace, is a sunken knot garden about 150 ft (45 m) square and planted with all the flowers and herbs that were to be found in sixteenth- and seventeenth-century manor-house gardens. One area is a foot maze made of low, clipped Box and gravel. There are Honeysuckle and Rose arbours for relaxation, statuary for visual pleasure and terracotta pots with traditional wooden hoops through which are trained old-fashioned Pinks.

THE CHELSEA PHYSIC GARDEN

Chelsea, London

THE CHELSEA PHYSIC GARDEN is the second oldest physic garden in England. It was established in 1673 on its present site by the Worshipful Society of Apothecaries. In 1722, Sir Hans Sloane, the Lord of the Manor of Chelsea, presented the garden to The Apothecaries' Company on condition that they gave 2,000 pressed and mounted plant specimens to The Royal Society at the rate of fifty per annum, and maintained the garden for 'The manifestation of the glory, power and wisdom of God in the works of Creation'. By 1795, some 3,700 herbarium sheets had come from the garden. Sloane stipulated that if it ever ceased to be a physic garden, the land should revert to his heirs. Today the garden contains 4,500 different botanical species laid out by family in Natural Order Beds based on a modified Bentham and Hooker System from *Ranunculaceae* to *Graminae*.

In 1732, cotton seed was sent from here to James Oglethorpe in America; he organized the colony of Georgia and established the cotton industry there. In 1733, the great Linnaeus visited the Chelsea Physic Garden to collect plants and dried specimens.

In one area there is a herb garden containing about 300 different species. This is planned on a regular grid of square and rectangular beds intersected by brick and grass paths, with a large Bay tree as a focal point at the end of the main path. The beds are categorized according to use: culinary, medicinal, fragrant and dyeing. They are all labelled with their common and botanical names so that it is an ideal place for students of horticulture who are interested in herbs to increase their knowledge and see the plants growing to maturity each summer. The Chelsea Physic Garden is now open to the public from April to October on Wednesday and Sunday afternoons from 2 pm to 5 pm. All visitors will be amazed to find almost four acres of tranquility so unexpectedly in the heart of London.

SACRED
TO THE MEMORY OF
WILLIAM BLIGH, ESQUIRE, F.R.S.
VICE ADMIRAL OF THE BLUE,
THE CELEBRATED NAVIGATOR
WHO FIRST TRANSPLANTED THE BREAD FRUIT TREE
FROM OTAHEITE TO THE WEST INDIES,
BRAVELY FOUGHT THE BATTLES OF HIS COUNTRY,
AND DIED BELOVED, RESPECTED AND LAMENTED,
ON THE 7TH DAY OF DECEMBER, 1817,
AGED 64.

THE TRADESCANT GARDEN
St Mary-at-Lambeth, London

JOHN TRADESCANT the Elder is one of the first English gardeners and plant collectors of whom we have considerable knowledge. Born *c.* 1570, he was gardener to Sir Robert Cecil of Hatfield House and to Queen Henrietta Maria, wife of King Charles I; Tradescant referred to her as 'The Rose and Lily Queen'. In 1637 he was appointed keeper of the Botanic Garden at Oxford, but died the following year. John Tradescant the Younger followed in his father's footsteps, and went to America plant collecting. Together they collected curiosities and rareties, which they showed in the first public museum in London, nicknamed 'The Ark', at John the Elder's house in Lambeth. This collection was subsequently acquired by Elias Ashmole and formed the basis for the Ashmolean Museum at Oxford.

Both Tradescants are buried at St Mary's-at-Lambeth, and the redundant church is leased to The Tradescant Trust as the headquarters of The Museum of Garden History. As a tribute to the Tradescants a 30 ft (9 m) square knot garden was designed in 1982 by Lady Salisbury, a descendant by marriage of Sir Robert Cecil. It is based on a design of interlocking circles and half circles of Box with a variegated Box shrub as a central point. In between the interlocking circles are placed three T-shapes of grey *Santolina incana*. The thirty-two other herbs planted are all ones that would have been known to the Tradescants and grown in gardens in England during the seventeenth century. On one side of the garden is the tomb of Captain Bligh of *The Bounty*, and in another corner a lion's head fountain splashes water into a basin, slightly disguising the sound of the London traffic, and making the garden an oasis of peace beside the gatehouse of Lambeth Palace and the busy Lambeth Bridge Road.

THE QUEEN'S GARDEN AT KEW PALACE

The Royal Botanic Gardens, Richmond, Greater London

THE ROYAL BOTANIC GARDENS at Kew were established by Princess Augusta, a daughter-in-law to King George II, at the time that Kew Palace was built at the end of the seventeenth century. Designed in the Dutch style, it was also lived in by King George III and Queen Charlotte, who died there in 1818. Behind the Palace are two gardens laid out in 1964 by Sir George Taylor, the then director of Kew, to complement the architecture of the house. Centred on the garden side there is a formal parterre 150 by 75 ft (45 by 23 m), whose formality mirrors the ceremonial of aristocratic life in seventeenth-century England.

The scented garden is 150 by 40 ft (45 by 12 m) and bounded on three sides by an arched Laburnum arbour. In the centre there is a gilded wrought-iron garden ornament in the style of Jean Tijou, balanced by two rectangular beds. These are separated by paths from the sloping beds that surround the whole area. At one end there is a Camomile-turfed seat backed with Box, which is also used as the edging plant for all of the borders. The garden is filled with a wide range of scented herbs and plants, many of which were used as strewing herbs in the sixteenth and seventeenth centuries. It was then the custom to cut fresh stems of Meadowsweet, Lavender, Artemisia or other highly scented herbs and to mix these with straw, which was then scattered on floors after they had been cleaned, to give a sweet aroma and to mask the smells of inefficient drainage. Kew is an inspiration to anyone wishing to create their own formal scented garden.

7 SAINT GEORGE'S ROAD

Twickenham, Greater London

Mrs Jenny Raworth is a professional arranger of both fresh and dried flowers, especially for weddings. Her garden in Twickenham is used to the maximum to produce plant material for her business. It is probably no more than a quarter of an acre, but within this somewhat limited space she has two herb gardens. The bee garden is laid out in the traditional way with two intersecting paths and a birdbath in the middle. The four beds have Box tree spheres at their centres and are bordered with low Box edging. She grows about fifty different types of herbs in this garden, specializing in many species of creeping Thymes. Bees also like visiting the Hyssop and Bergamots that grow here, and it is a short flight from the two hives in one corner. On the day we visited Mrs Raworth, the bees were in a very angry mood as she had just collected their honey. On more tranquil days it must be a delightful garden in which to sit; one scarcely realises that a main road connecting a motorway to central London is close by.

Immediately outside the kitchen is another formal garden, 24 by 18 ft (7.3 by 5.5 m), surrounded by an 8 ft (2.5 m) high horseshoe-shaped Yew hedge. There are two beds edged with Box and filled with Santolina. Four corkscrew Box trees are planted in terracotta pots and seats are arranged against the Yew curve from which this delightful small formal garden can be enjoyed.

HAM HOUSE

Richmond, Greater London

Ham House was built in the 1670s by the first Duke of Lauderdale. He was the richest aristocrat of that period and built the grandest possible house to impress his peers and to exhibit to the world the greatness of his position and the ostentation of his wealth. Almost every piece of carved wood or moulding was gilded, the walls were hung with velvets, damasks and tapestries and the rooms filled with elaborate furnishings, great beds, solid silver candelabra and imported china. The house remained in the Tollemache family almost undisturbed, until 1947 when it was given to The National Trust by Sir Lyonel Tollemache. By then most of the grandeur had decayed and the original formal gardens had entirely disappeared. The Trust has done its best to restore the interiors to their former grandeur and once more laid out the formal gardens around the house following as closely as possible the design shown in a late seventeenth-century picture that is on show in the house.

Beyond the garden front, avenues of Lime trees have been planted in a design reminiscent of formal French gardens. Immediately below the 200 ft (61 m) terrace is a long border planted only with Rosemary and Purple, Green and Golden Sage at regular proportional intervals. On the east side of the house is a parterre 135 by 120 ft (41 by 36.5 m). Along one side is a pleached Lime *allée*, and the rest is surrounded by a clipped Yew hedge. Two main paths cross on the diagonal, within which are four rectangular beds ornamented with pyramid- and cone-shaped Box trees at each intersection of the major and minor paths. Box is used as edging and the beds are filled with hundreds of clipped mounds of grey Cotton Lavender. Such gardens and parterres were very popular in the seventeenth and early eighteenth centuries, but almost all were swept away when the passion for more naturalistic gardening inspired by Capability Brown became the fashion.

THE ROYAL HORTICULTURAL SOCIETY
Wisley, Surrey

T HERE HAS BEEN a herb garden at Wisley for some years, although four years ago it was re-planned by David Palmer so that it would be more easily accessible to disabled visitors. It is surrounded by hedges of Hornbeam, *Phellodendron, Pyracantha* and Rosemary. There are four main paths of York stone set on the diagonal with a sundial set in brick as the focus. The garden is divided into four square sections crossed by small brick paths. One section is devoted to culinary herbs, the second to aromatic, the third to medicinal, and the fourth to dye plants and those herbs that have folklore associations. As centre points in the culinary and medicinal sections there are two terracotta urns rescued from a garden in Penge, in the London Borough of Bromley. There are about 225 different species and cultivars in the garden, and they are all clearly labelled for easy identification.

There is a dichotomy in any garden that tries to be both attractive and educational, since no one has yet solved the problem of labels that can be read easily yet do not dominate the garden scene. Wisley is therefore an interesting garden to visit in order to see a wide range of herb material, well identified and maintained, but it is clearly a demonstration garden lacking some of the subtle tranquil charm that is essential to any herb garden. The garden is set on high ground near the subtropical greenhouses, and it will be helped when the hedging, particularly the hedge of *Rosmarinus officinalis fastigiatus*, 'Miss Jessop's Variety', grows to form a more enclosed space, for this garden is visited by so many as their first introduction to planning a herb garden.

LEEDS CASTLE

Maidstone, Kent

Leeds Castle has been described as 'the loveliest castle in England', sitting in the middle of the gently rolling and romantic Weald of Kent landscape, surrounded by a wide moat on which glide roseate-beaked black swans. The castle was built in the thirteenth century and was restored in the 1920s by 'good old American money' and also 'good new American know-how', both supplied in quantity by The Hon. Lady Baillie, who came from the Whitney family. On her death The Leeds Castle Foundation was endowed as a centre for medical research and for residential conferences.

The old cutting garden covering one-third of an acre was re-planned in 1980 by the late Russell Page. The site is an oddly angled sloping area framed on three sides by stables, cottages and old high brick walls. The fourth side opens on to the valley of the river Len where a lake called The Great Water has been made. The overall plan is very simple. It is essentially a vast cottage flower garden formalized by the Box hedges surrounding the beds. Page wanted 'to enable you to walk this way and that through a field of flowers'.

It has been called The Culpeper Garden in honour of Lord Culpeper who owned Leeds Castle in the seventeenth century and was a relative of Nicholas Culpeper, the famous herbalist of that time. Herbs are used here mainly as contrasting foliage material between the flowers and the old-fashioned Roses. There is, however, a bed of culinary herbs for use in the castle kitchen. The garden also has The National Monarda or Bergamot Collection organized by The National Council for the Conservation of Plants and Gardens; there are five species and fifteen cultivars here. This new garden is generous in concept and a most attractive addition to the beauties of Leeds Castle.

 90

STONEACRE
Otham, Kent

THE HALF-TIMBERED manor house of Stoneacre nestles in a hidden valley which defends it from the approaching suburban sprawl of Maidstone. Built in about 1480, the northeast wing was added in 1920 and is constructed from the seventeenth-century timber framing of nearby North Bore's Place. Stoneacre now belongs to The National Trust and is cared for by Mr and Mrs Cecil Thyer-Turner, whose love of the place is reflected by their devotion to the house and its interiors and to the surrounding romantic gardens, which are filled with Roses and old-fashioned flowers creating a fairy-tale atmosphere. The plants are allowed to luxuriate and none more so than those in the Shakespeare Herb Garden.

Seven years ago this garden area, which is only 30 by 18 ft (9 by 5.5 m) and surrounded by Yew hedging, was a superior rubbish heap. But now it is filled with every herb Shakespeare mentioned in his plays, from wild Thyme rescued from its midsummer bank to Ophelia's Rosemary and Rue. There are many gardens dedicated to the Bard of Avon, but none is as successful as the one shown here. More than fifty types of herbs are grown, planted in irregular drifts so that the garden is a tumbling riot of scented and useful plants. Each plant must fend for itself and only the most robust survive; the weaklings go to the compost heap and are replaced each year. If your fantasy is to have a dreamy herb garden of complete informality, then search out this secret garden and be inspired by it to plant your own literary homage of Elizabethan herbs.

EYEHORNE MANOR

Hollingbourne, Kent

M R AND MRS DEREK SIMMONS bought this small fifteenth-century manor house and garden some years ago and it is now a shrine to her enthusiasm for herbs and all their uses, with a particular emphasis on the laundry. One of the rooms in the manor contains a unique Laundry Museum showing the equipment used by our ancestors to achieve the weekly clothes wash. This activity was, until recently, both labour intensive and exhausting, and we can only be relieved that modern appliances and associated products have made this task so much easier.

The garden is less than one acre and the herbs are grown in such profusion they spill out over the winding paths, so that finding one's way through the garden requires care. There is hardly space left for the garden seats, when one wants to sit and enjoy this abundance.

Saponaria officinalis, commonly called Bouncing Bet or Soapwort, which spreads with an invasiveness somewhat similar to Mint, has a prominent place here. The root of this plant was dug up, dried, slivered and made into an infusion (of one pound of root to one gallon of water), which served as the most effective cleaning agent known to our forebears. Soiled clothes were placed in this liquid, steeped for half-an-hour and then rinsed in a running stream until the water ran clear from the garments. The fabric so treated would be both clean and have regained its original colour and lustre.

Many other herbs are planted informally in this garden, and with climbing Roses growing over the low eaves of the roof one has a great sense of the abundance and generosity of nature.

IDEN CROFT NURSERIES AND HERB FARM

Staplehurst, Kent

Rosemary Titterington is an enthusiast. When she acquired Iden Croft Farm she started by growing soft fruit, but is now involved with growing herbs for every possible purpose: the wholesale and retail selling of plants; fresh-cut herbs for the catering trade all over England; edible flowers for special menus at a famous London hotel; and a range of fresh herbs for use in the cosmetics created for a firm that is a British household name. These are her current projects, but her fervour is such that tomorrow she may well take on fresh commitments to further stimulate her good self and her hard-working staff.

To show what herbs look like when they are mature she has planted a 40 ft (12 m) square garden display area that consists of four irregularly shaped beds separated by meandering paths. One bed on a rocky area is filled with aromatic herbs, with a special emphasis on creeping Thymes that particularly like a well-drained scree habitat. A second bed is filled with culinary herbs; the third is divided between dye plants and herbs such as Nasturtiums, Marigolds and Violets. The fourth bed has Mints at one end, medicinal herbs at the other and in the centre The National Collection of Marjoram, which has been assembled for The National Council for Conservation of Plants and Gardens and The British Herb Trade Association. Anybody can go to the nursery to identify almost any species of Marjoram, and be sure that their plant is of a named type. There is a shop which sells a wide range of herb products, and you are likely to encounter Rosemary talking non-stop to anybody who comes in, about her love of herbs. She is a mine of fascinating information about the 350 types of herbs that are for sale, and can occasionally be persuaded to part with one of the very special group of fifty herbs that are not yet on her price list.

SISSINGHURST CASTLE

Sissinghurst, Kent

T HE HERB GARDEN at Sissinghurst laid out by Harold Nicolson and Vita Sackville-West in 1938 is the oldest extant herb garden in England. All gardens by their very nature are impermanent and fashions in gardening have changed and modified amazingly over the centuries. It is this re-creation of a traditional herb garden which has inspired the design of hundreds of others now growing throughout Britain.

When the Nicolsons discovered Sissinghurst Castle it was a range of desolate and untidy farm buildings, the surrounding four acres littered with the barnyard detritus of a hundred years of neglect. It became their home in 1930, and Harold Nicolson designed the basic plan of Yew hedges, paths and garden areas, which Vita Sackville-West filled with her unique blend of rollicking flowers, shrubs, trees and climbers.

The herb garden is about 150 yds (137 m) from the Tower. It is an 80 ft (25 m) square, making one of the famous garden 'rooms' with its tall Yew hedges. The plan is almost symmetrical with a large Byzantine marble basin positioned where the two main paths cross at the centre of four square beds, around which are eight other large beds. There are now about eighty different herb species grown in the garden, although rarely more than three plants of each type are set out, yet there is enough herb material to make a good display and to allow for some variations. The planting takes great advantage of the individual characteristics of each type of plant, being arranged by size, form and colour. Houseleek fills the basin, butterflies hover over the rare white-flowered Borage, and the tall, daisy flower heads of the golden yellow Elecampane contrast wonderfully against the dark black-green of the Yew hedges, reminding one that traditionally it was this herb that was being gathered by Helen of Troy when she was abducted by Paris – a legendary herb plant in a legendary garden.

SCOTNEY CASTLE

Lamberhurst, Kent

S COTNEY is a dreamy meeting between nineteenth-century wealth and twentieth-century taste. There has been a moated castle at Scotney since 1378. In 1837, the Hussey family decided to build a new castle on higher ground overlooking the ruins of the original building. Today, a wide sloping glade filled with Rhododendrons and Azaleas connects the two buildings and leads down to the romantic old castle surrounded by its moat, which expands into a lake filled with Water Lilies, home to two black swans. Christopher Hussey, the important writer on English country houses, spent the last thirty-eight years of his life making these gardens – mainly with a restrained palette of plant material – into a vision of romance and beauty.

A courtyard of the old castle is partly in ruins with only the façade of the seventeenth-century banqueting hall and a small two-storey annex remaining. The hall wall is clothed with white Wisteria, a Box hedge at its base ; both are background to the circular herb garden. A well-head is placed in the centre of the lawn encircled by three borders containing about thirty different herbs. Many of these are variegated species, so that the gold-splotched and golden-tipped leaves add a contrast to the severe planting. White Tulips grow between the plants in the spring and old Roses cover the walls of the other parts of the courtyard, so that in high summer it looks like a faded antique tapestry waiting only for ghostly revellers to peer through the glassless windows. In the distance flocks of sheep graze on untroubled fields and today's visitor experiences a timelessness as the senses are enchanted by perfume, colour and calm. Across the moat in an island glade a shaft of sunlight reveals the sculpture – *Three Piece Reclining Figure, Draped,* 1977 – which is Sir Henry Moore's tribute to Christopher Hussey's genius.

BATEMAN'S

Burwash, East Sussex

R UDYARD KIPLING lived at Bateman's from 1902 until his death in 1936, and it was he who laid out the very English gardens that surround the house. It was built in 1634, and is now the property of The National Trust, who have restored the working mill, which again grinds flour, for sale to visitors to the house and the garden.

In an upper garden against a very long brick wall, Mr Woodbine Parish, the designer, has laid out a herb garden 80 by 6 ft (24 by 1.8 m). There is a Bay tree at one end that suffered badly in the long winter of 1984; established Bay trees are usually tough, but can succumb in adverse conditions. Young Bay trees will withstand most planting situations so long as they are protected from wintery winds in exposed positions during the first five years. It is therefore often sensible to grow them initially in large pots or Versailles boxes and to move them to a protected site during the winter months. In the right location Bay can grow to 60 ft (18 m) and so should be placed with some care if you do not wish your herb garden to be dwarfed forty years on.

At Bateman's, about eighty different herbs are massed together, and it is an excellent example of herbs used in a grand herbaceous border. In such a situation they must be grouped boldly and the plants tidied up from midsummer onwards if the garden is not to have an unkempt look in the latter part of the season.

MICHELHAM PRIORY

Upper Dicker, East Sussex

MICHELHAM PRIORY was founded in 1229 by The Lord of Pevensey and first colonized by Augustinian canons from Hastings Priory. Sometime before 1400 the great moat was dug within the existing bend of the river Cuckmere. The gatehouse was built after Henry VIII's Dissolution of the Monasteries, when two-thirds of the buildings were destroyed, the remaining structures being turned into a farmhouse that, from 1603 to 1897, became the centre of a 1,000 acre estate owned by the Sackville family. In 1959, the Priory with seven acres of land became the property of The Sussex Archaeological Society, and in 1981 a physic garden was laid out immediately to the south of the house, in which are grown plants that would have been used at the Priory during its medieval zenith.

The garden has an irregularly shaped bed in the centre, around which is another wide herb border enclosed by a Yew hedge. There are eleven medicinal planting areas: for rheumatism, gout and painful joints, Mugwort, Mustard and Lily-of-the-Valley; for use in the household, Sage, Soapwort and Tansy; for childbirth and children's diseases, Stitchwort, Horehound and Violet; for heart, lung and blood disorders, Plantain, Mullein and Coltsfoot; for wounds and broken bones, Self-Heal, Comfrey and Salad Burnet; for bites, stings, burns and poisons, Orris, Mallow and Calamint; for digestion, stomach and liver, Sorrel, Chicory and Rue; for depression and dreams, Poppy, Feverfew and Borage; for head, hair and skin, Fumitory, Love-in-a-Mist and Pennyroyal; for animal husbandry, Balm, Sweet Cicely and Chickweed; and for eyes, ears and teeth, Marigold, Wall Germander and Bistort. This enchanting small physic garden also has the only really well-designed labels that we have found, which are as amusing as they are informative.

DENMANS

Fontwell, West Sussex

FIVE YEARS AGO a fortuitous meeting took place between an elderly woman, who had made and nurtured a remarkable plantswoman's garden, and a young garden designer who had just left Iran in a hurry. For forty years Mrs Robinson had collected plants avidly, used gravel ground-cover to suppress weeds and enthused to everybody who came to the garden near the sea in West Sussex, on that device and her love of plants. John Brookes, well known from his books on garden design, is today a leading international landscape designer and teacher. He found his haven at The Clock House at Denmans, where he helps Mrs Robinson maintain and improve her garden in between his heavy schedule of designing gardens, giving courses and lecturing on garden design.

At Denmans he has created an informal herb garden within some old brick walls in an area 20 by 40 ft (6 by 12 m). Paving stones have been laid out irregularly, with a large stone jar as a central point. The paving encourages you to wander randomly through the garden, which contains about sixty different herbs planted informally, both for use in the kitchen and for their decorative qualities. The plants grow magnificently in this sun-trap, and it is a most pleasant place when the climbing Roses are in bloom on the walls, the butterflies drifting and the bees humming. It is fortunate that informality is the keynote, as five years ago one grey-leaved yellow Mullein was planted and has since self-seeded so successfully that its tall vertical flower heads now appear in the most unlikely places. Few herb gardens are planned with such studied disorder, but it is delightful to see how effective such a design can be when carried out by such a knowledgeable person.

COOKE'S HOUSE

West Burton, West Sussex

ON A VERY WET, cold March morning we visited Miss J.B. Courtauld to look at her herb garden. Before we could say anything other than our names, we were standing in front of a blazing fire in the library with cups of coffee, and as we thawed, were gently asked why we were there. Cooke's House is a fairly large seventeenth-century, stone building with some eighteenth-century interior decoration, well-polished furniture, wide bowls of potpourri and old oil paintings. Its owner, Miss Courtauld, is an enthusiastic plant lover and her parents had employed Gertrude Jekyll to help with the design of the garden in the front of the house; in 1909 it had been photographed for *Country Life.*

The herb garden is in one of the secluded gardens behind the house. It is about 50 ft (15.2 m) square and hedged on three sides by Rosemary. A path leads between two Lavender-filled beds and two standard Yews to the focal point marked by an urn. This is almost enclosed by two broken rectangular beds, one filled with Irises and the other with thirty different herbs. It is near enough to the kitchen to be convenient for the cook and also hidden from the rest of the garden, so that on a fine day in early June you look down the path, through the cloud of blue and yellow Iris flowers to the urn, and beyond to the 'borrowed' landscape of the softly rolling Sussex hills. This garden was laid out in 1963, but fits perfectly into the setting of the old house, long-established gardens and warm hospitality, which only generations of love can give to a house and its garden.

THE BUTSER ANCIENT FARM RESEARCH PROJECT

Petersfield, Hampshire

The Butser Ancient Farm Research Project exists to re-create a farm of the fourth century BC and to operate it by methods as close as possible to those of the Iron Age. As part of this project a herb garden is being created on a steeply rising site above the main agricultural areas. The area covered is 150 by 30 ft (46 by 9 m), and is positioned on a slight convex curve. Four terraces have been constructed, one above the other, supported by grass banks. These are divided into three units approximately 30 ft (9 m) long, separated by vertical walkways. There is not enough room for paths to be extended along each terrace. The plants are divided into different beds and, as far as is possible, placed vertically according to the time of their introduction into Great Britain, and horizontally by their usage.

The first two terraces are devoted to plants that were probably available in the Iron Age and are recognized from such archaeological evidence as carbonized and water-logged seeds, seed impressions on pottery and from identifying pollen. One of these beds is devoted to indigenous herbs that appear on the local South Down region of Hampshire. The third terrace is filled with herbs that would have been used in the Romano-British period and the fourth terrace contains herbs used today. More than 150 different herbs have been planted within these categories, and new species are continually being added. This herb garden is fascinating, not only because of its early historic references, but also because the four terraces, so boldly situated on their steeply sloping hill, should show any visitor that a splendid herb garden can be created in the most unlikely of situations.

THE TUDOR HOUSE
Southampton, Hampshire

T HE TUDOR GARDEN at Tudor House is the most accurate re-creation in England of what ornamental gardens were like from about 1485 to 1603. The area is 75 ft (23 m) square and in the centre there is a formal knot garden based on a design of interlocking squares and circles. Around this are placed formal rectangular beds bounded by 3 ft (90 cm) high railings supported by balusters. On one side two tall wooden columns painted in a chevron pattern support gilded heraldic beasts. Elaborate painted garden ornamentation was much used in Tudor times and can now only be seen in glimpses in the background of sixteenth-century pictures or in a mere handful of drawings and plans. The apogee of this type of garden decoration was in the fabled gardens of Nonsuch Palace (1538–1647). The painting of *The Family of Henry VIII*, c.1545, shows a bedizened section of the contemporary Great Garden at Whitehall Palace, through a background window. In 1979 this picture was used as part of the opening beat of *The Garden* exhibition at the Victoria and Albert Museum.

Mrs Sylvia Landsberg designed the Tudor Garden in 1980, including a fountain, an orchard, a close walk, herber or arbour and a secret garden with a niche for a bee skep. The planting is formal and includes thirty different herbs divided between the herb bed and the knot garden, with a hundred other plants that would have been available in Elizabethan times. At this period, plants were often given a symbolic meaning. Thus, Bay was associated with immortality, the Gillyflower with spirituality, Lavender with happiness, for it 'comforteth the brain', and Sweet Marjoram with virtue. It is a splendid reconstruction and exemplifies the care that our ancestors lavished on their gardens however small they might have been.

BEAULIEU ABBEY

Beaulieu, Hampshire

IN 1204, a major Cistercian abbey was founded by King John at Beaulieu, which in old French means 'beautiful place'. Little of it remained in 1870, when the estate was given to the first Lord Montagu as a wedding present, except for the dorter, chapel, gatehouses and cloister walls. He built Palace House over the monastic gatehouses and the current baron, Edward, has developed the estate and made it the setting for The National Motor Museum.

Ten years ago he asked the late Mrs Moyra Burnett and the Directors of Tumblers Bottom Herb Farm, to design and replant the beds around the wide cloister garth with herbs that would have been used in the monastic kitchens and infirmary. More than eighty different types were chosen and laid out in wide drifts to contrast with the ancient walls. On the north side a low wall was covered with variegated Ivy and therefore the bed below was planted with herbs that have gold variegated leaves: Golden Sage, Golden Thyme, Golden Marjoram, Ginger Mint and Golden Lemon Balm. On the other side of this wall, in a more shady position, are alternating masses of Lungwort, Lovage, Periwinkle, and the Stinking Hellebore. Centred on another wall is a magnificent *Magnolia grandiflora*, which means that the bed beneath it has dry, poor soil and gets little rain or sun. The herbs that have been found to flourish, with some feeding, in this inhospitable situation are Violets, Sweet Woodruff, Hart's Tongue, *Vinca minor*, Pennyroyal and Horehound.

Horehound is a traditional remedy for chest complaints and was also used in medieval times as a sweetmeat, since its candied roots were considered to be a great delicacy. Legend had it, and a tenth-century Swiss monk, Walafrid Strabo, admonished, 'Hoarhound is bitter to the palet, and yet sweet to drink. Drink Hoarhound hot from the fire if you are poisoned by your step-mother.'

THE ALLEN GALLERY

Alton, Hampshire

THE ALLEN GALLERY, housed in a group of sixteenth- and eighteenth-century buildings, contains pictures collected by William Herbert Allen (1863–1943), some of which were chosen, in 1941, by The Council for the Preservation of Rural England as suitable for a pictorial survey of England. The Gallery also exhibits its comprehensive collection of English ceramics dating from 1550, and the Tichborne Spoons, hallmarked from 1592, some of the most important Tudor silver displayed anywhere. Another benefit is the pleasant garden available for visitors to wander through after looking at the exhibitions. It gives the impression of having been there for centuries, although it is in fact a creation of the last ten years. More pertinently, a small courtyard space 20 ft (6 m) square was made into a herb garden only five years ago; an area similar in size to hundreds of thousands of town gardens.

There are buildings on two sides of the site and low brick walls on the other two sides. Faced with the problem of such a small area the designers decided to eliminate any grass and have only beds filled with herbs, stone paving and a sundial as a central incident. The garden appears to be formally laid out, but the beds are slightly irregular to accommodate the profile of the existing buildings. Within this tiny space, room has been found for seventy-six different herbs ranging from creeping Thymes to Angelica, and from Garden Mint to Meadowsweet Dropwort. All the herbs could be obtained from any herb farm, none are annuals and all can be used either in the kitchen, to scent rooms or as bases for simple home herbal remedies. Once planted, so long as the soil is well drained and the aspect sunny, such a garden needs remarkably little up-keep, and gives pleasure all the year round.

WEST GREEN HOUSE

Hartley Wintney, Hampshire

WEST GREEN HOUSE is a National Trust property, and has been rescued twice by the present leaseholder; once when he originally restored the house on taking the lease and again after a disastrous fire three years ago. It is an idyllic Georgian brick manor house with stone dressings, and on the formal front, in niches, there are marble busts of five Roman emperors who gaze out across the lawns and the wide fields beyond. The garden front has a small formal parterre made up of Box hedges, mop-headed standard Box trees and clipped Cotton Lavender. Outside the drawing-room windows there is a larger parterre with gravel paths, and beds, again edged in Box, filled with clipped herbs and some flowering annuals. In another area there is a Victorian re-creation of an Italian garden, with elaborate water-works, Baroque scrolls and statues.

The most exciting of the gardens is enclosed by venerable brick walls and is planned as an immense *jardin potager*, 300 by 100 ft (91 by 30 m). It is divided into two almost equal sections with 12 ft (3.6 m) wide wooden Chinoiserie gazebos, which are walled with bird-proof netting and used as splendid soft fruit cages. Radiating from these are eight large beds bordered by Box hedges and planted with serried rows of vegetables, chosen also for their decorative qualities, and interspersed with long ranks of different herbs carefully placed for their foliage and height. Large clumps of old-fashioned Roses are planted symmetrically to give colour and scent in late June and July. One is reminded inevitably of the formality at Villandry near Tours, but this garden has a much more domestic atmosphere than that great garden in France. This is the apogee of the romantic ideal of a vegetable plot that contains everything a cook might want, but also delights the eye.

FARNHAM ROYAL HERBS

Farnham Royal, Buckinghamshire

At The Chelsea Flower Show three years ago, we met Jessica and Jeremy Houdret, who had just planted a herb garden as an adjunct to their herb farm within the grounds of their house, next to the church at Farnham Royal. The house had once been owned by the builder of Hampton Court, Cardinal Wolsey's Principal Clerk of Works. Nothing remains of the clerk's garden, but now there are three different herb gardens. One is a long border, 30 by 9 ft (9 by 2.7 m), against a tall hedge, intersected by low walls and filled with aromatic and medicinal herbs arranged so that the various heights of the herbs used make an impressive composition of contrasting form and leaf shape. In planning a herb garden the mature height of plant material is possibly the most important consideration and this is well demonstrated by the skill that Jessica Houdret has shown in the planning of her long herb border.

The second garden is another wide herb border, and the third, a Rose and herb garden with a circular bed in the centre, is planted with herbs, such as *Nepeta cataria* and *Alchemilla vulgaris*, that have a particular affinity to Roses. A sundial is the focal point in this garden.

The herb plants grown for selling are laid out in an area approximately 100 ft (30 m) square as a *jardin potager*, or formal vegetable garden, divided by brick walks. The vegetable beds in this area are edged with herbs and there is a mop-headed Bay tree in the centre. Day courses are given during the summer at Farnham Royal and the students go away having seen and learned about the perfect combination of herbs laid out here both for decorative and commercial purposes.

HOLLINGTON NURSERY

Woolton Hill, Berkshire

THE HOPKINSONS of Hollington are becoming authorities whenever herbs are mentioned. Their herb farm in an old walled garden is a favourite haunt of the media, and Judith and Simon are frequently quoted when journalists want more information about herbs and their uses. The calm luxuriance of the display beds and the order of the growing beds, both within and without the polythene tunnels, belie the chaos they found ten years ago when the walled garden was a wilderness, and which they transformed during the early years of heroic endeavour that were necessary to establish this highly successful herb farm.

The couple further complicated their lives by choosing to have for several consecutive years a herb garden on the Rock Bank at The Chelsea Flower Show, for which they were determined to win a gold medal. The judges gave them that accolade in their fifth year at Chelsea, and they have since used the main elements of the winning design as the culmination point of the two 80 ft (24 m) display herb borders at the nursery. This design is of concentric circles, with a fountain in a pool at the centre. Around this is a circle of York stone paving, then large pebbles through which grow Ajuga, variegated Meadowsweet and Dwarf Comfrey, the whole being surrounded by a grass path. Judith's enthusiasm for the many species of Thyme is represented, and other herb plants are chosen for the strong contrast provided by their leaf shape or colour.

Growing plants for the five days of The Chelsea Flower Show is a nightmare that begins a year in advance. The plants chosen have to be coddled and nursed so that they will appear at their best in late May, a time which might be quite alien to their natural growing habits. This often means either forcing or retarding them so that they will present perfect specimens to beguile the judges.

HILLBARN HOUSE

Great Bedwyn, Wiltshire

Hillbarn House is a long low modest building on the main street in the pretty village of Great Bedwyn. Through a very small side door, one enters into a very large enchanting garden divided by high hedges, and with fine old trees. Adjacent to the house is a courtyard filled with flowers in beds and terracotta pots. Steps lead up to the garden, which was laid out in the 1960s with some assistance from the late Lanning Roper. One of England's foremost landscape designers, he helped plan the pleached Limes, *Tilia europaea*, and Hornbeams, *Carpinus betulus*, and the Lime tunnel.

In the upper part is the herb garden, 42 by 24 ft (128 by 7.3 m), which was designed and constructed by the owners in 1973. It is divided into two equal parts by a path; each of these sections being further divided into twenty beds, 2 ft (60 cm) square. The squares alternate between gravel and herbs, and each herb bed has a species standard Rose planted in the middle. In June, when the Roses are in full bloom, a veil of scented colour drifts above the herb plantings. Each square is planted with a single herb chosen to contrast with its neighbour. Chequerboard gardens can be monotonous, but the addition of the standard Roses to the pattern gives the basic design a splendid vertical variation. The planning of gardens need not be a complicated exercise but it is essential to have one dominant incident and then to allow the herb planting to enhance that. The herb garden at Hillbarn House shows how successful the design can be when carried out by gardeners who have patience, love and enthusiasm.

YOUNG HOUSE

Wootton Rivers, Wiltshire

A FEW YEARS AGO at a garden centre we overhead Mrs Nancy Young buying twenty plants each of several different herb species. When asked, she said that they were to complete a small herb garden she had started, with the help of Graham Carr, the previous autumn in the walled courtyard of a sixteenth-century West Country cottage she had just restored. The herb garden is 50 ft (15 m) square. The design is formal: four beds in the centre with their inner corners cut out to form a circle for the Box tree in the middle. These beds are surrounded by twelve more, and all are edged with clipped Box hedging. Planting is restrained and the herbs are kept meticulously trimmed, only a few being allowed to flower in order to maintain the formality. The exceptions are ornamental Rhubarb and Foxgloves, which are allowed to grow to full height. Eight of the beds have 4 ft (1.2 m) high terracotta pots that were made specially in Italy. Gravel paths provide the background and the contrast to the planting.

The garden appeared mature and well-established six months after it had been planted, and three years later it looked as though it had always been there. Timbers from a 350-year-old barn have been used to make a two-storey dining room overlooking the herb garden, plate glass in-fills rather than a rendered wattle-and-daub surface making a stunningly dramatic room. With a guest house on the other side of the courtyard, this enchanting garden can be seen and appreciated from every part of the house and its annexes. Planned to show the contrasting leaf shapes of the plants and the other architectural elements, the strict formality of the design makes the garden as attractive in the winter, when it is mainly defined by the Box edging and the terracotta pots, as it is in June and July, when it is a geometric pattern of greens and greys.

THE AMERICAN MUSEUM

Claverton Manor, Avon

IT WAS the inspiration of an American, Dr Dallas Pratt, and an Englishman, the late Mr John Judkyn, to establish, in 1960, The American Museum outside Bath, to be the only museum in Europe where people could see the artifacts that were made in North America from the mid-sixteenth to the end of the nineteenth centuries. Claverton Manor, a large though not palatial house, was designed in 1820 by Sir Jeffrey Wyatville in a restrained late-Georgian style. The house has been brilliantly adapted to take the visitor chronologically through the era covered by the collection; as a treat at the end of the tour, one can eat freshly baked cookies from an original American Colonial kitchen called Conkey's Tavern. It was shipped lock, stock and stove to the museum from Massachusetts.

A small herb garden, 21 by 16 ft (6.5 by 5 m), is placed just beyond the main south terrace overlooking the heavily wooded Avon valley, and was donated by the ladies of The Southampton Garden Club of New York. Designed by the director, Mr Ian McCallum, the garden contains about fifty different herbs that would have been grown in an eighteenth-century American herb garden. The interesting thing is that almost all the herbs grown, with the exception of Bergamot, or the American Indian Oswego Tea, would have been found in English herb gardens of the same date; the herbs are those that would have been used in cooking, for medicine and scent. The garden is surrounded by a cobbled path edged with Box. In the middle is a traditional American garden focal point, a dome-shaped straw bee skep enclosed by Wall Germander and Cotton Lavender, which are two herbs particularly loved by bees. More herbs are used in the reconstruction of part of George Washington's garden at Mount Vernon, Virginia, and both gardens add to the many amazing pleasures of an afternoon at Claverton Manor.

R.T. HERBS
Kilmersdon, Somerset

WE FIRST MET Mr Richard Taylor almost thirteen years ago when we had just started a herb nursery. He not only helped us on the herb farm but also put in most of the plants when we designed the herb garden at Woburn Abbey. He also spent many months helping to renovate our nearby house. Mr Taylor is a man of many parts; he had been growing his own herbs behind his house about a mile away and in 1983 he set up his own herb farm on land adjacent to the original nursery. He and his wife Alice now grow about 130 herb varieties, many of them propagated from Tumblers Bottom Herb Farm stock plants, the botanical chain continues.

Next to the propagating greenhouse he has laid out an extensive display garden, 90 by 42 ft (27 by 12.8 m). The central area contains neat rows of healthy herbs in containers and at either end a mass of other plants are allowed to grow to their full maturity. Beyond this bed is a 40 ft (12 m) square within which is a generous circle of paving stones. This is filled with *Rosa gallica*, Lavender in variety, Artemisias, Lovage, Angelica, Feverfew, Evening Primrose and Elecampane. In high summer this bed makes an amazing show of different colours, scents and foliage with the tall plants adding dramatic emphasis to the design. These display gardens demonstrate how easy it is to create an apparently mature effect with herbs in only two seasons. Using the correct choice of plants, such a scheme could be realised in any new garden and give a most satisfying result in a short time. Seeing the gardens here should encourage many first-time gardeners to use these charming and most rewarding plants.

HESTERCOMBE HOUSE

Cheddon Fitzpaine, Somerset

THE GARDENS of Hestercombe House are possibly the finest creation of the collaboration between Miss Gertrude Jekyll and Sir Edwin Lutyens. They designed a vast enclosed sunken garden, The Great Plat, to lie below the south front of the house. Above and along the far side is a long Rose-covered pergola from which there are splendid views over the fields and woods of Taunton Vale to the Blackdown Hills. Work on the garden started in 1904 and by the time the estate was acquired in the 1950s to be the headquarters of the Somerset County Council Fire Brigade, the gardens were decaying sadly. This organization was far-sighted enough to institute the restoration, partly from plans by Miss Jekyll's own hand found pinned inside a potting shed on the estate and, more importantly, from other plans discovered among the Beatrix Farrand Collection in the archives of the Landscape Department of the University of California, Berkeley. The serious re-creation began in 1975, and it was completed five years later, so that one can now see and enjoy one of the few authentically restored and re-planted large-scale Jekyll/Lutyens gardens.

At the far end of Lutyens's magnificent orangery, a double flight of steps leads up to the raised Dutch Garden, a fine example of his skill in using an unpromising patch to brilliant advantage. The mound it occupies was an old rubbish dump that was to have been removed completely. It was paved, a circular bed placed in the middle and surrounded by four cruciform beds with two further beds against the back wall on either side of a garden gate. The formal beds are planted with Roses, Yucca, Lavender and Nepeta and all the beds are edged with *Stachys lanata* or Lambs' Tongue, some of Miss Jekyll's most favourite and most used plants.

CRANBORNE MANOR

Wimborne, Dorset

CRANBORNE MANOR was built by King John as a hunting lodge in 1207. Its present appearance owes much to King James I's great minister, Robert Cecil, the first Earl of Salisbury, who re-built the house in about 1610 and gave it the enchanting fairy-tale image that it has today.

Lady Salisbury, then Lady Cranborne, went to live there in 1954. It was here that she developed her great horticultural skills and re-created the gardens to mirror the beautiful house. One of the most important of these is a herb garden, about 100 by 30 ft (30 by 9 m) and surrounded on three sides by ancient high Yew hedges. Rectangular *clairvoyées* have been cut in them so that one can glimpse the wooded 'captive' landscape beyond. The garden is divided into six large rectangular beds bordered by Cotton Lavender. A sundial on a plinth has been placed as a focal point where four of the grass paths meet. This is encircled by standard Honeysuckles, which have become a Cranborne and Hatfield House garden trademark. The beds are filled with about eighty different herbs, informally planted and encouraged to grow to their full splendour. It is the quintessential English herb garden.

Outside the library Lady Salisbury has recently made a seventeenth-century knot garden, 80 by 30 ft (24 by 9 m). There is a circular bed with a topiary corkscrew Box tree at its centre. This bed is surrounded by eight beds laid out in geometric patterns, all edged and divided with Box. Lady Salisbury in *The Englishwoman's Garden*, writes 'I have had a lot of fun with the knot garden, here I have been a purist and grown only plants used in the sixteenth and seventeenth centuries. Friends, generous and kind, have given me ancient Pinks, Rose Plantain, the Double Sweet Rocket and gold-laced Polyanthus and they grow with Gerard's Double Primrose and Plumed and Double Hyacinths and the stately Crown Imperial without which no early knot was complete.'

A GLOSSARY OF HERBS

ACONITE
Aconitum napellus
Herbaceous perennial

FAMILY Ranunculaceae
HEIGHT 3 ft (1 m)
FLOWERS Dark blue; early to mid
   summer
SYNONYMS Monkshood, Wolfbane,
   Auld Wife's Huid

Aconite is one of the most poisonous plants found growing in the wild. It may not be native to Britain but it is mentioned in manuscript herbals from the tenth century. The name Wolfbane comes from the Greek, *lycotonum*, for Greek warriors used Aconite juice on their arrowheads, to kill wolves. In medieval times the herb was known as Monkshood, because of the cowl shape of the flower. The dried root is designated as a Class I poison and must be treated with much respect.

Aconite likes damp soil and thrives best in shade. Prepare the area the autumn before planting; the soil must be well dug and preferably have been broken up by the first frost. Add a good compost or well-rotted manure to the soil. Increase by root propagation in the late autumn by transplanting the scion roots that will have developed during the summer. Aconite is also raised from

seed sown in a cool greenhouse or cold frame in early spring but care must be taken that the correct seed is planted; twenty-four varieties of Aconite have been classified. It takes between two and three years to come to maturity from seed.

Aconite was once used as a sedative and painkiller, but is now prescribed externally in herbal medicines. It is definitely not recommended for use in simple herbal home remedies.

ANGELICA
Angelica archangelica
Biennial

FAMILY Umbelliferae
HEIGHT 6–8 ft (1.8–2.4 m)
FLOWERS Greenish-yellow; mid to
   late summer
SYNONYMS Garden Angelica, The
   Root of the Holy Ghost

Angelica is native to northern Europe and Asia. It was said to have been introduced into Britain from *c.*1568. In the region of Poland once known as Pomerania, it was carried in processions by peasants chanting an ancient ditty – so antiquated as to be unintelligible even to the singers themselves – that was probably a survival from some pagan rite. The connection with Archangel is two-fold: firstly because Angelica is said to bloom on the feast day of St Michael the Archangel, and secondly because in the seventeenth century John Tradescant the Elder brought it to Britain from Russia where he found it growing near the city of Archangel.

Angelica is best grown from seed, but since that rapidly loses its viability it should be sown as soon as it is ripe, in mid autumn, in deep moist soil. Plant out the seedlings 3 ft (1 m) apart the

following year. The plant is a biennial, but if the seed heads are cropped in the first year it should continue to grow for several years.

The large fleshy stems, cut into sections and boiled in a sugar solution several times and dried, make crystallized Angelica used for confectionery. The seeds are used as a flavouring for the liqueurs Benedictine and Chartreuse.

APOTHECARY'S ROSE
Rosa gallica officinalis
Perennial

FAMILY Rosaceae
HEIGHT to 3 ft (1 m)
FLOWERS Light crimson; early to
    mid summer
SYNONYMS Rose of Provins, The
    French Rose

Botanical authorities maintain that
Persia was the original country of the
cultivated Rose. *Rosa gallica's*
distributory migration extended across
the Middle East and Asia Minor to
Greece and then to Italy and southern
France. The word Rose comes from the
Greek word, *rodon* meaning 'red'. *Gallica*
is one of the three major mother
strains for all the Roses grown today,
and the largest group of Old Shrub
Roses. The French called it *Rose de Provins*
and its early commercial applications
included use as a colourant base for
medieval rouge.

The Apothecary's Rose is an
extremely useful garden plant. It is
almost thornless and makes an
excellent hedge; mid-winter pruning is
best. Although it has a much shorter
flowering time than its many modern
offspring, the exquisite blooms and
their rich powerful fragrance more

than compensate. This Rose will not do
well in shade or partial shade, but it will
grow in any poor soil.

From the petals of this and other
Roses comes the unique flavouring for
two splendid French liqueurs – *Parfait
Amour* and *L'Huile de Rose*. The culinary
uses of Roses are many and honey of
Roses, Rose wine, Rose and fruit salad,
Rose jam and Rose petal jelly are just a
few of the delightful Rose recipes that
have been popular for centuries.

BASIL
Ocimum basilicum
Tender annual

FAMILY Labiatae
HEIGHT 20 in (50 cm)
FLOWERS White; mid to late
    summer
SYNONYMS Sweet Basil, Royal Herb

Basil is native to India and is widely
grown in most tropical and sub-tropical
countries of the world. It was known
throughout ancient Egypt from where
it was distributed to the countries of
the Mediterranean basin; the strong,
spicy flavour and clove-like scent were
admired by the Greeks and Romans. It
was first grown in Great Britain in the
sixteenth century and in North
America in the 1700s. Basil is associated
particularly with the cookery of the
south of France and Italy.

Classed as a tender or half-hardy
annual, in northern climates the only
means of propagation is by seed sown in
the spring. Use a sandy compost and
the trays or pans should be well
protected by a frame, greenhouse or
some form of cloche. Good air
circulation, full sunlight and a dryish
heat are important for successful
germination, which should take about
fourteen days. The seedlings are highly

susceptible to 'damping-off', a fungal
disease encouraged by overcrowding
and too-wet conditions in the seed
trays or pots. Damping-off can be
prevented by sowing the seeds thinly
and widely, watering the seed trays or
pots with a proprietary fungicide, and
guarding against an over-humid
atmosphere. Plant out in growing
positions after all danger of frost is past
and encourage bushiness by picking out
the main stem at 6 in (15 cm).

BAY or SWEET BAY

Laurus nobilis

Evergreen shrub or tree

FAMILY Lauraceae
HEIGHT 30–60 ft (9–18 cm)
 depending on climate
FLOWERS Pale yellow; late spring or
 early summer
SYNONYMS Nobel Laurel, Poet's
 Laurel, Roman Laurel, Bay Laurel

When growing in its native Mediterranean habitat, Asia Minor and southern Europe, Bay becomes a tree of up to 60 ft (18 m), but in Great Britain, northern Europe and North America it is usually seen at a maximum height of 15–30 ft (4.5–9 m). Because its neat habit suggests formal shapes, Bay is often clipped into standard or pyramid forms about 4–6 ft (1.2–1.8 m) tall, and grown as shrubs in pairs of decorative tubs or singly at the focal point of the traditional square herb garden. The botanical names are from the Latin *laurus*, 'to praise', and *nobilis*, 'famous'.

Laurus nobilis is an evergreen, with aromatic lanceolate leaves which are smooth, shiny, mid to dark green and 2–4 in (5–10 cm) long. It flourishes in coastal regions where it is frequently used for hedges. In cold climates Bay should be planted in a sunny sheltered position as it can be damaged by frost and winter winds. Propagation is easily done by layering or more often by cuttings taken of half-ripened shoots. Nurserymen suggest that rooted cuttings prefer to be pot-bound during the juvenile years. Bay is known for being slow growing.

BORAGE

Borago officinalis

Hardy annual

FAMILY Boraginaceae
HEIGHT 24 in (60 cm)
FLOWERS Blue; late spring to early
 summer
SYNONYM Burrage

Borage is native to Mediterranean regions, but it has been naturalized all over Europe. Borage self-seeds at such a fecund rate that it is now considered to have been a garden-escapee. According to Pliny, Borage was the legendary herb *Nepenthe*, mentioned by Homer, which when macerated in wine brought absolute forgetfulness. The genus name is thought to have come from the Latin word *buria*, meaning 'a flock of wool', for Borage is entirely covered with short hairs. In the seventeenth century John Evelyn described this herb's benefit as follows: 'Sprigs of Borage are of known virtue to revive the hypochon-driac and cheer the hard student.'

Borage seeds freely and thrives in full sun in almost any soil that is fairly well drained. A first sowing of seeds is recommended during spring or when the ground is beginning to warm up. Happily, when a garden has the herb Borage it is likely always to have it in some corner or other. Bees like it because its nodding flowers are pendulous, which prevents the nectar from being washed away by rain. The leaves taste vaguely of cucumber and are traditionally added to summer drinks such as Pimm's Cup. The beautiful flowers are often candied for decorating food. A tisane of Borage is popular in France for the relief of fevers and pulmonary complaints.

CATMINT

Nepeta cataria
Perennial

FAMILY Labiatae
HEIGHT 12–24 in (30–60 cm)
FLOWERS Blue; mid to late summer
SYNONYM Catnep

Catmint is native to Europe and Asia and is found all over the southern part of England growing in hedgerows, at the edges of fields and in waste ground on chalky and stony soils. It is now found wild in North America, where it was introduced. Its scent, which is similar to Pennyroyal and Mint, has a powerful allure for cats. They will roll on and destroy any plant that has been bruised, but never seem to trifle with a plant grown from seed. There is an old saying:

If you set it, cats will eat it
If you sow it, cats don't know it.

Catmint can be increased from cuttings taken in the summer, by dividing the roots in the spring or autumn, or it can be grown easily from seed sown in the spring. It does not need as much moisture as, say, Mint and prefers a sunny position. The pleasant grey-green leaves and bluish flowers make catmint a very pretty border plant and

it is a good contrast to shrub Roses. The dried leaves are used in a tisane to aid sleep, and were at one time smoked to cure throat complaints, until it emerged that this use had a slight hallucinatory effect.

CHERVIL

Anthriscus cerefolium
Biennial

FAMILY Umbelliferae
HEIGHT 24 in (60 cm)
FLOWERS White; early to late summer
SYNONYMS Garden Chervil, Beaked Parsley

Chervil is native to eastern Europe and western Asia; some sources give southern Russia as its native land. The Greeks were said to have used it as a herb flavouring and the Romans cooked it as a vegetable on its own. Records show that Chervil was grown as a popular herb for *sallets* (salads) in sixteenth- and seventeenth-century England, the seeds being even more important than the leaves for this. It was not used much in the eighteenth and nineteenth century, but it is now being cultivated more widely both in America, where it is an introduced plant, and in Britain, but France is where Chervil is most loved. Chervil's species name has a Greek derivation, *chairephyllon*, 'herb of joy' or 'pleasing foliage'.

The leaves of Chervil are finely cut, lacy and a bright shiny green. The tiny white blooms are formed at the top of

the flower umbels, a characteristic of this family, which includes Parsley and Fennel. Chervil is strictly classed as biennial; seed sown in late summer will over-winter to provide an early spring crop. Otherwise it should be approached as an annual with successive sowings made through the growing season until a patch has been established when it will self-sow readily from year to year.

CHIVES

Allium schoenoprasum
Hardy perennial

FAMILY Liliaceae
HEIGHT to 12 in (30 cm)
FLOWERS Dark pink; mid to late
  summer
SYNONYM Cives

Chives are the smallest and most delicately flavoured cultivated form of *Allium*, the Onion genus, and are a close relative of Garlic, Shallot and Leek. The plant is a native of temperate northern Europe and is distributed from southern Europe to Siberia and North America, now growing wild in Canada and the United States. The species name is a Latin derivation from Greek root words, *schoenos*, 'rush' and *prason*, 'leek'.

The 'grass' of Chives is a clump of hollow, smooth grey-green spears. The flower heads should be nipped off to keep the Chives tender and to stimulate growth from the small bulbs. Plants can be raised from seed, but for a quicker return buy clumps and divide them in the autumn or spring, planting them 2 in (5 cm) deep and 8–9 in (20–22 cm) apart. Chives should always be cut and not pulled. Make progressive cuttings to within 2 in (5 cm) of the

ground. In time a new crop of the delicious spears will appear. However, the plants should be regularly fed. Remember that being bulbs, Chives need some top growth for strengthening and regeneration, so do not cut away all the leaves.

CLOVE PINK

Dianthus caryophyllus
Perennial

FAMILY Caryophyllacae
HEIGHT 12 in (30 cm)
FLOWERS White, pink or red; early
  to mid summer
SYNONYMS Clove, Gillyflower,
  Carnation, Sops-in-Wine

The Clove Pink came originally from the Mediterranean and may have been introduced to Britain by the Normans. The genus name *Dianthus* is from the Greek words, *Di*, 'Zeus' or 'Jove' and *anthos*, 'flower', the complete meaning being 'the flower of the gods'. The genus name *caryophyllus* comes from an Indian folk name meaning 'fruit of the clove' and refers to the scent of its petals. Unusually, the colour name 'pink' is derived from the flower name, rather than the other way around. Gillyflower comes from the French word, *girofle*, meaning 'cloves'. Sops-in-Wine refers to the medieval tradition of the petals and flower heads being scattered on top of wine cups or cordials to impart a taste of cloves. The petals of Pinks can be candied by painting them with stiffened egg white and then dusting them with powdered sugar. Dried Pink petals are also used as

an ingredient in potpourri.

Clove Pinks were always cultivated in medieval gardens either in clumps or as edging plants, and have continued to be grown in cottage gardens up to the present day. It is from this variety of *Dianthus* that all other Pinks and Carnations have been developed. It can be grown from seed, cuttings, side-layering or root division, and likes a sunny, well-drained situation.

CORIANDER

Coriandrum sativum
Half-hardy annual

FAMILY Umbelliferae
HEIGHT 12—36 in (30—90 cm)
FLOWERS White; early to mid
summer

Coriander is indigenous to the countries of the Mediterranean and Caucasus and is now a weed in many places. It was used in ancient Egypt and also by the Greeks and is mentioned by Sanskrit authors. Its name is derived from the Greek word *koros*, 'a bug', since the plant smells strongly of insects, some say bedbugs. The inhabitants of Peru are so fond of the taste and smell of Coriander that they put it into almost all of their cooking. The seeds are used as a flavouring for certain liqueurs.

Coriander is grown from seed sown outside in spring. It can be slow to germinate, but the fresh leaves should be ready for cropping from early summer onwards.

Coriander adds a very distinctive taste to salads, and is an ingredient of the Mexican avocado dish, *Guacamole*, and of the cuisines of China, India and most of the Mediterranean countries. This herb is unusual in that while the

leaves have a sour, soapy taste, the scent and taste of the seeds are vaguely of orange. The seeds are now widely available particularly in Asian and Indian speciality stores and delicatessens, and perhaps would be more widely used if, like the Chinese, we believed that they bestow immortality.

COTTON LAVENDER

Santolina chamaecyparissus
Perennial

FAMILY Compositae
HEIGHT 24 in (60 cm)
FLOWERS Yellow; mid to late
summer
SYNONYM Santolina

Cotton Lavender or Lavender Cotton is not a true Lavender. It has clustered dense button flowers and very finely cut grey leaves. Other forms are *Santolina incana*, and its grey dwarf form called *nana*; another grey type *S. neopolitana*; and *S. virens*, a pretty green *and* evergreen form. The *incana* form along with Box and Wall Germander are three of the most popular herbs for outlining formal herb gardens and parterres. Reasons for this are their neatness of habit, favourable response to severe pruning and their hardiness. Santolina makes neat little grey hedges; it is also often used in the making of 'tussie-mussies' and nosegays. It is a native of southern Europe and distributed from Dalmatia through to Northern Africa.

Cotton Lavender is easily propagated from cuttings 2–3 in (5–7.5 cm) long, taken as the plant starts to grow again in mid spring. Dip the cut ends in a rooting compound and put them into

seed trays. The cuttings root very easily and can be planted out when they are 4–5 in (10–12 cm) high in well-drained soil in full sun. Cotton Lavender hedges should be clipped in mid spring. Well-established Cotton Lavender plants can become very woody and should be pruned vigorously if they are to remain a well-shaped plant or hedge.

DANDELION
Taraxacum officinale
Perennial

FAMILY Compositae
HEIGHT 12 in (30 cm)
FLOWERS Yellow; early spring to
mid autumn
SYNONYMS Priest's Crown, Swine's
Snout, Pissenlit

Dandelion is seen in all areas of the
northern temperate zone, but it is not
native to the southern hemisphere. It
grows on grazing land, open land and
on uncultivated ground and is
generally looked on as an ubiquitous
weed. It blooms in early spring and
exuberantly scatters its seeds during the
growing season. It is also one of the
most helpful of all European herb
plants. The word Dandelion is a hybrid
from the French term, *dent de lion*. The
herb has always been prescribed for
renal, liver and stomach problems. The
young leaves have been used as a salad
ingredient and the roots, dried, milled
and roasted, make a reasonable
substitute for coffee, while the flowers
brew up into Dandelion wine.

Although Dandelion appears very
freely in its wild state, if it is intended
for use in the kitchen, then it should be
grown from seed sown out in moist,

rich soil in the autumn. The roots take
between one and two years to develop
fully, and can then be harvested for
either culinary or medicinal purposes.
It is best to collect the parts to be used
from healthy vigorous plants and if
gathered from wild plants, these should
be growing well away from main roads.

ELDER
Sambucus nigra
Perennial

FAMILY Caprifoliaceae
HEIGHT to 30 ft (9 m)
FLOWERS White; early to mid
summer
SYNONYMS Pipe Tree, Bore Tree,
Black Elder, Common Elder

Elder is native to Europe, North Africa
and West Africa; elsewhere it is an
introduction. It was long thought to be
sacred, and was also supposed to be the
tree from which Judas Iscariot hung
himself. In England today, hedgers and
country folk are sometimes unwilling
to cut an Elder if it is found by the
wayside. *Aeld* is the Anglo-Saxon for
'fire', and the hollow stems of the
young branches were used by Ancient
Britons for blowing out fires. They were
also used as pipes; hence its name of
Pipe Tree or Bore Tree. Gypsies still
refuse to burn Elder in their communal
fires.

Elder is easy to propagate from
suckers or cuttings taken in spring or
autumn; it prefers a damp situation. Its
medicinal uses are legion: treatment for
catarrh, colds, constipation and as a
gargle. The leaves are made into an
ointment for bruises and the flowers

into cosmetics and used as a medium
for mixing medicines for eye and skin
lotions. Elderflowers impart a muscat
flavour and are used to make
Elderflower wine and Elderflower
'champagne'. Elderberry jelly and wine
are also excellent.

EVENING PRIMROSE
Oenothera biennis
Biennial

FAMILY Onagraceae
HEIGHT 3–4 ft (1–1.2 m)
FLOWERS Yellow; early summer to
mid autumn
SYNONYMS Tree Primrose, Common
Evening Primrose

Native to the eastern part of North America, Evening Primrose was first introduced to Italy and from there was distributed throughout Europe. The genus name comes from two Greek root words, *oinos*, 'wine' and *thera*, 'the hunt'. In North America it is viewed as a weed while in Britain it is considered a pretty garden plant. The unusual and unique botanic habit of the Evening Primrose is that the large satiny yellow, sweetly scented flowers open in the early evening and show themselves for only one night. Each flower lasts only a short time, but the plant produces masses of buds over a long period.

It has been discovered that Oil of Evening Primrose is effective in the treatment of many degenerative diseases of the nervous system such as Multiple Sclerosis, and can relieve the symptoms of pre-menstrual tension.

The cultivation of Evening Primrose

is simple, given a sunny and sandy situation. Like many herbs it will grow almost anywhere. It usually comes true from seed, and a plant allowed to run to seed in the second year will produce a considerable batch of self-sown seedlings the following spring. These can be lifted and planted out.

FENNEL
Foeniculum vulgare
Hardy perennial

FAMILY Umbelliferae
HEIGHT to 5 ft (1.5 m)
FLOWERS Yellow; mid to late
summer
SYNONYMS Fenkel, Sweet Fennel,
Wild Fennel

Fennel is another of the culinary herbs native to southern Europe and the shores of the Mediterranean. Its history is as ancient as the Egyptian papyrus documents in which Fennel is mentioned. It was used both by the Romans and the Anglo-Saxons. It grows wild in Europe and in most temperate countries and is now a naturalized plant in California as well. Fennel thrives on limestone-based soils and is most partial to chalky sea-cliff situations. Cultivated Fennel is a much sturdier plant than the wild form, which has thin, spindly stems and leaves.

The mature height of Fennel makes it an excellent plant for the background of a border or as a focal point in a traditional formal herb garden. The delicacy of its feathery leaves and its umbels of exquisite tiny yellow flowers is wonderfully decorative. It is easy to

grow in any soil and sunny situation from seed sown in spring or early summer, or as soon as the soil is warm enough for outdoor sowing. The seedlings should be thinned out to about 12 in (30 cm) apart; the thinnings can be transplanted to other parts of the garden.

FEVERFEW
Chrysanthemum parthenium
Perennial

FAMILY Compositae
HEIGHT 24–36 in (60–90 cm)
FLOWERS White; mid to late
  summer
SYNONYMS Pyrethrum, Featherfew,
  Feather Foil, Flirtwort

Feverfew is a native of southeastern Europe and has been introduced into Britain and North America. It can be found growing in the wild on dry sites and well-drained soil. Its common name comes from the Latin word *febrifugia*, meaning 'a substance that drives out fevers'.

Feverfew has mid-green leaves and daisy-button flowers. It seeds freely, or can be propagated either by root division, cuttings, or by seed sown early in the spring and planted out in early summer. It likes a stiff loamy soil enriched with good manure.

The most recent interesting use of this plant is to treat the dreadful malady, Migraine. Research has been carried out at Chelsea College, London, which shows that relief has been obtained within six months by 70 per cent of the panel who ate one to five fresh leaves a day. As the leaves have a

musty taste like the smell of old chrysanthemums, it is not pleasant and occasionally some people develop minor mouth ulcers. But, a fresh sprig of a pleasantly flavoured herb such as Thyme or Sage used with the Feverfew leaf in a small sandwich makes this most effective herbal remedy more palatable. A tisane from the leaves has been employed for centuries as a tonic and as a medicine for rheumatism.

FOXGLOVE
Digitalis purpurea
Biennial

FAMILY Scrophulariaceae
HEIGHT 3–5 ft (1–1.5 m)
FLOWERS Pinkish-purple; mid
  summer
SYNONYMS Witches' Glove, Fairy
  Glove, Gloves of Our Lady, Bloody
  Fingers, Fairy Caps, Fairy Thimbles

Foxglove grows throughout Europe and is a common wild flower in Britain, seeding freely in woods and hedgerows, from Cornwall to the Orkneys. The Foxglove gets its name from the flower shapes, which resemble the fingers of gloves, and the deep woods where it grows were thought to be the haunt of fairies.

In 1776, William Withering found *Digitalis* was an effective treatment for dropsy. More recent investigations of the plant discovered the glycoside, digitoxin, which in small amounts is extraordinarily effective in regulating heart rate, rhythm, tone and contraction. Digitoxin is found in the leaves and research has not yet established why it is so effective for the treatment of heart disorders, but it is a poison and must be used only under strict medical control.

Foxglove grows best in well-drained loose soil with its roots in the shade and its flowers in the sun. It can be grown easily from seed sown in the spring, which will flower in the second year. But once established, the dense root structure will sustain growth and plants will produce flowers for several years.

FRENCH TARRAGON
Artemisia dracunculus
Herbaceous perennial

FAMILY Compositae
HEIGHT 18–24 in (45–60 cm)
FLOWERS none in northern zones,
  rarely sets seed
SYNONYM Little Dragon

True French Tarragon comes from southern Europe, and being a member of the Artemisia tribe is closely related botanically to Southernwood, Mugwort and Wormwood. It is thought to have originated in southern Russia and eastern Europe, but centuries of cultivation have resulted in the French Tarragon superseding its pale and tasteless Russian relative in the kitchen. Tarragon was brought to Great Britain in about 1548, and the first North American records for its introduction are dated *c.*1806. The derivation of the botanical name is *artemisia*, the Greek goddess of the hunt, and *dracunculus*, from the Latin for 'little dragon'.

  Tarragon enjoys sunshine and warmth and grows best in a light, dry, well-drained, rather poor soil. It needs protection in severe winters if left out in the open garden. Straw, bracken, chopped bark, peat and even plastic

sheeting pegged down over, and a coupled of feet around, the root area all help it survive to resume growth in the spring. If the winter is extremely harsh, then it is best to lift the roots and transplant them to a protected frame or to a large pot, to over-winter in a glasshouse or conservatory.

HEMLOCK
Conium maculatum
Perennial

FAMILY Umbelliferae
HEIGHT 5–6 ft (1.5–1.8 m)
FLOWERS White; mid summer to
  mid autumn
SYNONYMS Kex, Spotted Corobane,
  Beaver Poison, Poison Parsley

Hemlock is found in Europe and in temperate Asia and North Africa; it has also been introduced to North and South America. It is a member of the great order of *Umbelliferae*, the same family of plants as Fennel and Parsley and Queen Anne's Lace, which are also found growing in the wild. The identifying botanical feature is the purplish marking on the stem.

  Hemlock grows in neglected meadows, and on waste ground and by the edges of streams. It prefers a damp situation and grows readily in the wild but it is not a plant that most people would want to grow extensively in their gardens. All of it is deadly.

  Hemlock is one of the most ancient known poisons. It was the Hemlock juice that Socrates was forced to drink. Pliny wrote that it was good as an external for treatment for tumours. According to one legend the purple streaks on the stem symbolize the brand put on Cain's brow after he had murdered his brother.

LAD'S LOVE
Artemisia abrotanum
Perennial

FAMILY Compositae
HEIGHT 6 ft (1.8 m)
FLOWERS Yellow; mid to late
summer
SYNONYMS Old Man, Maiden's Ruin,
Boy's Love, Southernwood,
Appleringe

This splendid plant is native to
southern Europe, chiefly Italy and
Spain. It is a cousin of Mugwort and
Wormwood of the same genus. The
name Southernwood comes from the
old English for 'woody plant from the
south'. The name Lad's Love is
explained by the plant's ancient
reputation as an aphrodisiac. It is a
strongly camphor-scented plant with
an ability to repel insects. It is dried and
used by the French as a moth repellant;
they call it *Garde Robe*. Three medicinal
uses are as a tonic, enema and
antiseptic. Traditionally a bunch of
Southernwood was placed at the side of
the prisoner in the dock to prevent the
spread of jail fever.

Lad's Love is easily propagated from
young green cuttings in the summer or
from heeled cuttings taken from old
wood in the autumn; it can also be

grown from seed. Plant in full sun and
a light to medium soil with added
compost, and clip it hard in mid spring
to prevent ragged growth. It is an
excellent herb to grow for foliage in an
herbaceous border and for flower
arranging.

LADY'S MANTLE
Alchemilla vulgaris
Perennial

FAMILY Rosaceae
HEIGHT to 18 in (45 cm)
FLOWERS Yellowish-green; early to
late summer
SYNONYMS Lion's Foot, Bear's Foot,
Nine Hooks

Lady's Mantle is indigenous to the
Andes, but is now found all over Britain
and is sparsely colonized throughout
Europe, North America and parts of
Northern Asia, especially in the
Himalayas. In the medieval period it
was dedicated to the Virgin Mary,
hence the name Lady's Mantle, but it is
also called Lion's Foot from its
spreading, wide, palmate leaves. It is a
most attractive garden plant, with
pleated grey-green leaves, which
charmingly catch the early dew or rain
along their serrated edges and sparkle
in the morning sun beneath the
powdery clusters of pale lime-green
flower heads.

Propagation is either by root division
in spring or autumn, or by seed in the
spring. It is a prolific self-seeder, and
can pop up in paving cracks and similar
inhospitable places, and is happy to
grow in either full sun or partial shade

and in almost any soil. Traditionally, it
was an old simple for female
complaints, for which it is still
prescribed by modern herbalists. The
plants make a good edging to a border,
and its flowers and leaves are used for
floral decoration.

LAVENDER
Lavandula spica
Perennial

FAMILY Labiatae
HEIGHT 3 ft (90 cm)
FLOWERS Purple; mid summer to mid autumn
SYNONYMS Old English Lavender, Spike Lavender

Lavender is a shrubby plant, indigenous to the mountainous regions of those countries bordering on the western half of the Mediterranean. It has been grown in Britain for hundreds of years and the climate in this country produces a Lavender with the best essential oils; the finest Lavender grown commercially is *Lavandula vera*. Dried Lavender flowers, Lavender oil, Lavender water are three of the delicious products from this beautifully perfumed herb.

Lavender is fairly easy to grow so long as the soil is light, and it is planted in a dry, open, sunny position. It requires good drainage and freedom from dampness in the winter. If the roots are waterlogged for too long a period they rot and the plant dies. Lavender may be grown from seed sown in trays in late spring; plant out when the seedlings are 3 in (7.5 cm)

high. Green cuttings, $2\frac{1}{2}$ in (6.5 cm) long, taken in the spring or hardwood cuttings taken between early spring and late autumn can be used to increase stocks. After its third year the centre of a Lavender bush becomes woody; vigorous pruning in the early spring helps to maintain a good shape, but take care not to cut into the old wood. Lavender hedges should be pruned in this manner if they are to make an effective border.

LEMON VERBENA
Lippia citriodora
Half-hardy shrub

FAMILY Verbenaceae
HEIGHT 15 ft (4.5 cm)
FLOWERS Pale purple; late summer
SYNONYM Herb Louisa

This tender deciduous shrub was first introduced to Britain in the eighteenth century. It is only half-hardy, but can reach a height of 12–15 ft (3.5–4.5 m) in sheltered situations. Lemon Verbena is best planted near a south-facing wall, either against a house or near or in a conservatory so that the exquisite lemon scent can float through open windows and doors, filling the rooms on a hot summer day.

Lemon Verbena is always grown from rooted cuttings either from green cuttings 2–3 in (5–7.5 cm) long taken in the spring or from woody cuttings in late summer or autumn. As it is half-hardy new plants need protection from frosts and should be kept in a pot for their first two years of life, to be taken indoors or into a greenhouse during the winter. The shrub can often appear to be dead in the spring, but if the winter has not been too severe it will eventually break into bud again.

The leaves should be collected in late summer before they start to wither and dried in a dark airy place. They can then be used either for making a tisane for indigestion or, more especially, as a marvellous addition to potpourri. Lemon Verbena leaves retain their scent for many years, and the distilled oil is an essential basic ingredient in many perfumes.

LOVAGE
Levisticum officinalis
Herbaceous perennial

FAMILY Umbelliferae
HEIGHT 6–7 ft (1.8–2 m)
FLOWERS Yellow; early to mid
summer
SYNONYMS Old English Lovage,
Italian Lovage, Cornish Lovage

Lovage is a native of southern Europe, but has distributed itself in Asia Minor, Britain and the eastern United States. The genus name is a corruption of its earlier botanical name, *Ligusticum*, which came from Liguria, the name of the region in Italy where Lovage grew abundantly. The Greeks chewed the seeds to help digestion and to counter flatulence, and it was once grown widely in country gardens for its root, which was used for simple herbal home remedies and in cooking. According to the seventeenth-century herbalist, Nicholas Culpeper, 'The leaves bruised and fried with a little hog's lard and laid hot to any blotch or boil will quickly break it.' It is the eponymous flavouring in a country cordial called Lovage, which is still found in pubs in Cornwall and the West Country.

Lovage seed can be sown as soon as it is ripe in the summer in a sunny position in a well-manured, moist, well-drained soil. As with most herbs it does not like heavy clay. Lovage can be propagated by root division in the autumn and spring and will reach its mature height in two to three years.

This herb tastes very strongly of celery and can be used as a substitute when a recipe calls for the stalks, seed or salt of that vegetable. The flavour is very strong and it should be used most sparingly in soups and stews.

MEADOWSWEET
Filipendula ulmaria
Perennial

FAMILY Rosaceae
HEIGHT 3 ft (1 m)
FLOWERS Creamy white; early to
late summer
SYNONYMS Queen of the Meadow,
Bridewort, Lady of the Meadow,
Dolloff

The name Meadowsweet is derived from the earlier 'meadwort', since it was once used to flavour the beverage mead. This herb is one of the best known British wild flowers, decking out meadows and moist banks with fern-like foliage and tufts of delicate, graceful, creamy white flowers. The leaves are dark green and almond-scented, having quite a different fragrance to the flower, which is lemon-scented; both are dried for use in potpourri. Traditionally Meadowsweet was used as a strewing herb, to be spread on floors to disguise the odours of inefficient drainage. John Gerard wrote in his *Herbal* of 1597, 'the leaves and flouers of meadowsweet farre excelle all other strowing herbs for to decke up houses to strawe in chambers, halls and banqueting-rooms in the summer-time, for the smell there of makes the heart merrie and joyful and delights the senses.'

Meadowsweet is found in the wild, often growing in profusion in moist fields and in roadside ditches. It can be propagated from seed sown in the spring or by root division, also in the spring. Plant in damp, rich soil and partial shade for best results. Water well in dry weather.

MINT or SPEARMINT
Mentha spicata or *Mentha viridis*
Perennial

FAMILY Labiatae
HEIGHT up to 24 in (60 cm)
FLOWERS Pale pink; early to mid
  summer
SYNONYMS Garden Mint, Mackerel
  Mint, Green Mint, Fish Mint,
  Lamb Mint, Our Lady's Mint

The mint tribe is indigenous to
southern Europe and the
Mediterranean regions. It was one of
the several common culinary herbs
brought to northern Europe by the
Roman legions.

Most Mints have these basic
characteristics in common: square
stems; opposite single leaves; white to
purple flowers formed in clusters;
invasive habit; all are perennial.
Spearmint increases rapidly by means of
a creeping root system. Like all mints it
is invasive and the best way to deal with
it is to plant well away from other
herbs, including other mints. There are
several methods for checking the
invasive growth, such as planting in
sinks or plastic buckets from which the
bottoms have been removed (although
the life of plastic containers will be
limited), or by making enclosures of

sunken roofing tiles, slates, metal strips,
or tubs. Roots lifted at the end of
summer, planted in boxes and kept in
the greenhouse will produce fresh
shoots for use in the kitchen in early
spring. A separate patch of Black
Peppermint is useful for Mint tea.

MULLEIN
Verbascum thapsus
Biennial

FAMILY Scrophulariaceae
HEIGHT 5–7 ft (1.5–2 m)
FLOWERS Yellow; mid to late
  summer
SYNONYMS Our Lady's Flannel,
  Torches, Aaron's Rod, Shepherd's
  Stalk, Hag's Taper

Mullein has colonized throughout
Europe, Western Asia as far as the
Himalayas, and in North America
where it is a widespread naturalized
weed in the eastern United States. In
Britain it is found in hedgerows,
roadside verges and in waste ground,
especially where there is sand, pebbles
and chalk. In the first year it shows
only as a rosette of large thick, felted
leaves 6–12 in (15–30 cm) long, similar to
Dandelion. During the second year a
single robust flower stem shoots from
the centre of the rosette; for this habit
it is called Aaron's Rod. It was known
as the Candlewick plant because the
stem made excellent taper tinder when
very dry, and the name Hag's Taper
also refers to that use and to the grand
spikes of blossom, which resemble tall
candelabras.

Mullein can be grown from seed

early in the spring and it will be found
to self-seed very freely in the garden. It
does not thrive in wet, cold conditions.

Mullein is used as a physic with
many other herbs for the treatment of
chest complaints, and the dried leaves
are put into herbal smoking mixtures.
It is a wonderfully decorative plant and
adds a vertical interest to any
herbaceous border, but in that situation
care should be taken to remove
unwanted seedlings.

PARSLEY
Petroselinum crispum
Hardy biennial

FAMILY Umbelliferae
HEIGHT 10–12 in (25–30 cm)
FLOWERS Yellow; late summer
SYNONYMS Parsele, Petersylinge

Parsley has been called a native of the eastern Mediterranean, Turkey, the Lebanon and Algeria, but it has proved so adaptable it will grow in almost any climate. Linnaeus wrote that it was introduced into Britain from Sardinia during the sixteenth century. It was undoubtedly brought to America by the early settlers from Europe. The botanical name is a Latin derivation from Greek words, *petros*, 'rock' or 'stone', and *selinon*, 'parsley'.

Parsley has been called the universal herb and must be included in any kitchen garden, the ideal patch being near the kitchen door or in a pot on a sunny windowsill. Parsley should be grown in large quantities whatever the situation. Parsley seed is slow to germinate as the outside husk is quite hard. Fresh seed that is not more than one year old should be sown in late spring when the soil is warm. Good, deeply dug, non-acid soil is best, with dressings of organic fertilizer and soot

added, as well as amounts of powdered chalk; the prepared bed should be moist and raked to a fine tilth. A light sandy soil often produces weak plants, a good loamy, slightly clay soil is better. Gather a few leaves from each plant, rather than rob one plant of its growth.

PEPPERMINT GERANIUM
Pelargonium tomentosum
Tender perennial

FAMILY Geraniaceae
HEIGHT 12–24 in (30–60 cm)
FLOWERS White; early to late summer

Most scented Geraniums, or more accurately, Pelargoniums, are indigenous to South Africa. This large genus was introduced into Britain from the Cape of Good Hope *c.* 1632, but were virtually ignored until the late 1840s, when their usefulness in perfume manufacture was discovered by the French. After this they were widely grown as indoor plants, and in Victorian times were placed on wide staircases so that the scent would be released when the leaves were brushed by ladies' crinolines. The scents of different Pelargoniums range from peppermint to apple to lemon to rose.

In northern climates, all Pelargoniums are tender and must be kept indoors during winter. Therefore, it is sometimes more convenient to keep the plants in their pots and to plunge these into the flowerbeds during the summer, bringing them in again before the first frost. Propagation by root cuttings is easy if taken in late

summer and struck in a peat and sand mix. Any good potting mixture can be used in their permanent containers; it should be kept moist and the plants fed occasionally.

The leaves can be dried for potpourri and fresh leaves are used to flavour Apple jelly or cakes, by putting a few leaves on the bottom of the tin before the cake mixture is added.

PERIWINKLE
Vinca major
Evergreen perennial

FAMILY Apocynaceae
HEIGHT Prostrate, spreading to 24 in (60 cm)
FLOWERS Blue; mid to late spring
SYNONYMS Joy of the Ground, Cockles, Blue Buttons, Hundred Eyes, The Flower of Death

This plant is a European native and is found in mixed woodlands in well-drained loamy soil. It is disputed by botanists whether or not *Vinca* is native to Britain, but Chaucer described it prettily as the 'Fresh Pervinke rich of hue'. There are many superstitions surrounding the Periwinkle: in England the country folk thought of it as a talisman against the Devil; in Italy it was placed on the coffins of dead children; and in France it is a symbol of friendship. It obviously had many and various uses as shown by these lines from *The Boke of Secretes of the Vertues of Herbes, Stones and Certaine Beasts* by the thirteenth-century German philosopher, Albertus Magnus: 'Perwynke when it is beate unto pouder with worms of ye earth wrapped about it and with an herbe called houslyke, it induceth love between man and wyfe if

it bee used in their meals . . .'
Periwinkle is propagated by root division or stem cuttings taken in either spring or autumn. It is easy to grow, and makes an excellent ground cover. It prefers shady situations but will grow in full sun. There is also the much smaller-leaved *Vinca minor*, and there are some gold and silver variegated species, which can beautifully lighten a shady corner. Medicinally, Periwinkle has astringent qualities.

PINEAPPLE SAGE
Salvia rutilans
Perennial

FAMILY Labiatae
HEIGHT 24–36 in (60–90 cm)
FLOWERS Scarlet; mid to late summer

Native to Mexico and Guatemala, this Sage is sub-tropical, and must be protected from frost during the winter. Therefore, in temperate climates it is basically a house plant and on a sunny windowsill can keep its leaves throughout the year. The plant can be trained in a Bonsai style, and may live many years, the old stems finally becoming very woody. However, we have also seen it planted out in sheltered London gardens where it survives for some years outdoors in a shielded position.

Cuttings, 3–4 in (7.5–10 cm) long, taken in the summer will root quickly in a sand and peat compost; dust the 'heel' or 'node' with a hormone rooting compound and trim each leaf by one-third of its length before putting the cutting into the compost.
The long lush green leaves have a strong pineapple scent which is delicious and refreshing. The dried leaves can be added to potpourri.

POKE ROOT

Phytolacca americana
Perennial

FAMILY Phytolaccacea
HEIGHT 3—7 ft (90 cm—2 m)
FLOWERS White; early to mid
 summer
SYNONYMS Virginian Poke, Poke
 Berry

The herb is a North American native, found from New England south to Texas and Florida; in Europe it is now naturalized in the Mediterranean countries, thriving on light, rich soils, particularly in newly cleared land, field margins and roadsides. It is a handsome plant with spear-shaped racemes of flowers, about 6—7 in (15—17 cm) long, which become covered with purplish-red berries in the autumn. The name Poke Root comes from its American Indian name, *pocan*. Medicinally the main property is narcotic — it is used for cases of chronic rheumatism — and it has chemical constituents that are employed immunologically. Poke Root is also thought to contain a substance that is effective against the African snail that carries the debilitating disease, bilharzia.

Poke Root is found in the wild, but it can be propagated by seed sown in the

spring or by root division in autumn and spring. It prefers sunny positions in deeply dug, rich, well-drained soil. It makes a most dramatic plant in any garden and because of its height it should be positioned in the background of a border.

ROSEMARY

Rosmarinus officinalis
Evergreen shrub

FAMILY Labiatae
HEIGHT up to 6 ft (1.8 m)
FLOWERS Pale blue; spring and late
 summer
SYNONYMS Compass Weed, Polar
 Plant

Rosemary is native to southern Europe, Asia Minor and along the Mediterranean coasts; it grows best by the sea but will grow inland and is found even in regions of the Sahara. The botanical name is a Latin derivation: *ros*, 'dew', and *marinus*, 'sea', becomes 'dew of the sea'.

The common Rosemary is a dense, evergreen shrub with spiky foliage and clusters of pale blue flowers, much loved by bees. It is a very aromatic plant, and on a hot day the fragrance is of pine needles. There are white- and pink-flowered forms, and *R. officinalis aureus* has leaves mottled golden yellow.

The herb does best in light, rather dry soil and with some shelter from winter winds, but it will grow in any type of well-drained limey soil. In extreme northern climates, or where soil is badly drained it is best to grow Rosemary in a pot near a south- or

west-facing wall and over-winter it in a greenhouse or indoors. Put a good layer of crocks in the pot to provide adequate drainage. Do not cut branches if there is any chance of frost, as the plant would be damaged or even killed. Rosemary can be used for low hedges, trained against walls, and the form *R. lavandulaceus* makes good ground cover under Old Shrub Roses if protected in winter.

SAGE
Salvia officinalis
Evergreen shrub

FAMILY Labiatae
HEIGHT 24 in (60 cm)
FLOWERS Mauve; late summer
SYNONYMS Sawge, Broad-leafed
Sage, Garden Sage

Sage is native to southern Europe and to the north as far as Austria, growing in protected situations on dry limestone soil. The genus name *Salvia* is derived from the Latin *salveo*, meaning 'to save or heal'. In 1568 William Turner, the great English herbalist, wrote that it was effective to plant Rue among the Sage to 'prevent the poison which may be in it by toads frequenting amongst it, to relieve themselves of their poison, as it is supposed, but Rue being amongst it they will not come near it'. In Buckinghamshire and many other English counties if Sage grows robustly it signifies that the wife controls the house; a very old English proverb says,

> He that will live for aye
> Must eat sage in May.

Sage is best propagated from tip cuttings taken in the late spring or early summer, but it can be raised from seed. It enjoys dry soil and full sun. To encourage leafiness, mature plants should be cut back vigorously in late spring, after some cuttings have been taken.

Sage is mainly used today in cookery. It is equally good fresh or dried and complements rich meats such as pork or goose. It is sometimes used to flavour cheese, such as English Sage Derby. Sage-leaf tea was once popular, and a single leaf rubbed over teeth and gums was an early dentifrice.

SORREL
Rumex acetosa
Perennial

FAMILY Polygonaceae
HEIGHT 12–24 in (30–60 cm)
FLOWERS Greenish-red; late spring
to mid summer
SYNONYMS Green Sauce, Sour Crabs,
Cuckoo Sorrow

Sorrel grows wild throughout Europe, Asia and the Arctic regions, and has become naturalized in America. The Egyptians used the plant, and the Romans were known to have served it as a contrast to rich dishes. In sixteenth- and seventeenth-century England it was one of the basic salad herbs, both at the court and with the country folk. Sorrel would have been among the herbs taken and planted in New England by the early colonists. The name Sorrel is derived from its twelfth-century French name, *surele*.

Garden Sorrel has broad, arrow-shaped leaves 4–6 in (10–15 cm) long, the flowers appearing on an 18 in (45 cm) stalk rising from the centre of the leaves. It can be increased by either seed or division in spring or autumn, but seeds sown in early spring in rich, damp soil in either a partially shaded or sunny position, will produce the best

plants. Transplant when the seedlings are about 2 in (5 cm) tall, setting them 10–12 in (25–30 cm) apart. Sorrel is self-seeding, but the flower heads should be nipped off to encourage leaf growth. If allowed to go to seed then the patch will have to be renewed periodically.

The sharp-tasting leaves are an agreeable addition to summer salads and winter vegetable soups. A green sauce of Sorrel and Spinach is delicious with trout or salmon.

SWEET BRIAR
Rosa rubiginosa
Perennial

FAMILY Rosaceae
HEIGHT 3–6 ft (90 cm–1.8 m)
FLOWERS Pink; early to mid summer
SYNONYM Eglantine

Sweet Briar, with its cousin the Dog Rose, is found in open woods, in hedgerows and in cottage gardens; it likes the alkaline soils of southern England.

This Rose has always inspired great poets. Chaucer allowed,

That gave so passing a delicious smelle
According to the Eglentere full welle.

Shakespeare wrote in *Cymbeline*,

The leaf of eglantine whom not to
    slander,
Outsweetened not thy breath.

Sweet Briar Rose can be propagated from cuttings or, eventually, by root division. It likes any sunny well-drained position in the garden. Since all Roses are gross feeders, an annual top dressing is a good idea. The flowers are almost scentless, but are followed by bright coral hips in the autumn. Sweet Briar's unique quality for any garden is the wonderful rosy fragrance produced from the sweetly scented leaves; this is best just after a summer rain shower. Ideally this Rose should be planted near a house or garden room. If bushes are planted close together, it can be grown as a good intruder-proof hedge, for its mature habit is very dense and the stems are covered with excellent thorns. Sweet Briar can be trimmed in the late winter, but the blossoms will be less the following summer.

SWEET MARJORAM
Origanum majorana
Half-hardy annual

FAMILY Labiatae
HEIGHT 24 in (60 cm)
FLOWERS White or pink; late
    summer
SYNONYM Knotted Marjoram

Sweet Marjoram is native to the Mediterranean, Portugal, North Africa and the Middle East. *Marjorana* is a very old name of unknown derivation by which the plant was first known when it was introduced into Europe in medieval times. The common name Knotted Marjoram, refers to the unusual knot-like shape of the flower heads. In seventeenth-century England dried leaves and flowers of this herb were used in sweet powders and sweet washing waters.

In northern climates, Marjoram must be grown from seed each year. It is sensible to sow a first crop in a greenhouse in early spring, and to sow another crop outside in late spring when the soil is beginning to warm up.

Like all members of the genus, the leaves have a spicy, aromatic scent, and are excellent freshly cut and added to salads or any pasta dish. The leaves of Sweet Marjoram can be dried, though they do not have as strong a flavour as the leaves of Wild Marjoram, *O. vulgare*, which is the Italian *Oregano*. Pot Marjoram, *O. onites*, is perennial but the scent and flavour of Sweet Marjoram is better and makes the effort of growing it from seed each year worthwhile.

THYME
Thymus vulgaris
Hardy perennial

FAMILY Labiatae
HEIGHT 4–12 in (10–30 cm)
FLOWERS Pale mauve; late spring to
    late summer
SYNONYMS Garden Thyme,
    Common Thyme

Thyme is indigenous to all the countries bordering the Mediterranean; the stony hillsides of southern Europe, North Africa, Asia Minor and the Middle East are where it is to be found growing wild. It was grown and gathered by the ancients to flavour food, and was burnt as part of ceremonial rituals by the Greeks and Romans. The genus name is a Greek derivation: *thymum*, 'to burn sacrifice'.

There are many forms of Thyme; creeping varieties make neat mounds and upright types like common Garden Thyme form good low-growing hedges. Thyme thrives in a sunny, open, well-drained, limey soil. In heavier clay soils it is not so happy, and the flavour will not be as pungent. Thyme is essential to any herb garden and should be kept clipped back or its woody habit can take over and the herb will have to be replaced every three or four years. Seed,

cuttings, root division and layering are the ways of propagating it. Mature Thyme plants will self-seed and the seedlings can be lifted and transplanted. Alternatively, seed can be sown in the open ground in shallow drills and the seedlings thinned out for the garden or window-boxes. Division of two- to three-year-old plants can be done in spring. Thyme is a fine rock garden and edging plant.

VALERIAN
Valeriana officinalis
Perennial

FAMILY Valerianaceae
HEIGHT 5 ft (1.5 m)
FLOWERS Pink; early summer
SYNONYMS Setwall, Capon's Tail, All
    Heal, Great Wild Valerian

Valerian is native to Europe and northern Asia and is now found in North America; it grows in damp moorlands, ditches, meadows and near streams. There seem to be few references to Valerian in classical times, but it was so highly regarded as a herb in medieval times that it was given the name of All Heal. Chaucer mentions this herb in *The Miller's Tale*.

He himself as swete as is the roote
    of Lokorys, or eny cetewale.

It was used by the Anglo-Saxon herbalists and by Arab physicians at the early medieval medical institution, The School of Salerno.

Valerian is often found in the wild, and can be propagated by root division in the spring and autumn, or by seed sown in the spring. It enjoys a moist, dense loamy soil. Herbalists use Valerian for cases of nervousness and neuralgia; during the First World War it was employed to treat shell shock and nervous strain caused by air raids. Tisane of Valerian also helps to induce sleep. Because of its height and substantial flower heads it is a good plant to use elsewhere in the garden, as well as in the herb border.

WINTER SAVORY and
SUMMER SAVORY
Satureia montana and *S. hortensis*
Annual (Summer Savory)
Perennial (Winter Savory)

FAMILY Labiatae
HEIGHT 12 in (30 cm)
FLOWERS White or pink; early
summer

Both Savorys are native to southeastern Europe and North Africa, but have been introduced to Britain, America and elsewhere. The Romans counted both species to be amongst the most fragrant of herbs, and suggested that they be grown near beehives.

Winter Savory is grown either from seeds sown in spring or by cuttings or root division. It is a low-growing shrub, keeping its leaves throughout the year, and is one of the most useful herbs we have in the kitchen. Summer Savory is annual and must be grown from seed each year. It is ready for use in early summer and should not be allowed to flower if it is to maintain its flavour. Both Savorys are delicious in salads and omelettes and they have a particular affinity with beans – sprigs should be added during cooking. The dried leaves of either herb can be used as an alternative for Thyme.

YARROW
Achillea millefolium
Perennial

FAMILY Compositae
HEIGHT 3 ft (90 cm)
FLOWERS White to pale pink; early
to late summer
SYNONYMS Milfoil, Nose Bleed,
Soldier's Woundwort, Devil's
Nettle, Bad Man's Plaything

Yarrow is widespread throughout Europe, and will grow anywhere: on motorway verges, waste ground, railway yards and in meadows. The genus name *Achillea* is derived from the Greek war hero, Achilles, who allegedly used it to heal his soldiers' wounds during the siege of Troy. *Millefolium*, the species name, refers to its very finely cut foliage. The vernacular name, Yarrow, is a corruption of the Anglo-Saxon word, *gearwe*, which meant 'ready to heal'. Its traditional use for staunching blood, effected by Yarrow's high tannin factor, defines some of the common names.

Yarrow can be propagated by dividing the roots in either the spring or the autumn, although more conventionally minded gardeners classify it as a weed since it grows under even the most adverse conditions.

Yarrow tea is a good remedy for colds and headaches. Its common name, Devil's Nettle, connotes its use in divination and witchcraft. The ancient Chinese text of prophecy, *I Ching* (*The Book of Changes*) is consulted properly, not by throwing three coins, but by spilling fifty-two dried Yarrow stalks.

GARDENS OPEN TO THE PUBLIC

Gardens open to the public for at least six months of the year are listed below. Their opening days and times can be found in *Historic Houses, Castles and Gardens in Great Britain and Ireland* (British Leisure Publications). Gardens open only occasionally are listed in The National Gardens Scheme annual guide, *Gardens of England and Wales Open to the Public*. Both publications are available at newsagents.

ABBEY HOUSE MUSEUM
Leeds, West Yorkshire

ACORN BANK
Penrith, Cumbria

ALLEN GALLERY
Alton, Hampshire

AMERICAN MUSEUM
Claverton Manor, Bath, Avon

BARNSLEY HOUSE
Barnsley, Cirencester, Gloucestershire

BATEMAN'S
Burwash, East Sussex

BEAULIEU ABBEY
Beaulieu, Hampshire

BUTSER ANCIENT FARM
RESEARCH PROJECT
Petersfield, Hampshire

CHELSEA PHYSIC GARDEN
166 Royal Hospital Road, London

CRANBORNE MANOR
Cranborne, Wimborne, Dorset

DENMANS
Fontwell, West Sussex

EMMANUEL COLLEGE
Cambridge, Cambridgeshire

EYEHORNE MANOR
Hollingbourne, Kent

GAINSBOROUGH'S HOUSE
Sudbury, Suffolk

HAM HOUSE
Richmond, London

HARDWICK HALL
Chesterfield, Derbyshire

HARLOW CAR GARDENS
Harrogate, North Yorkshire

HATFIELD HOUSE
Hatfield, Hertfordshire

HESTERCOMBE HOUSE
Cheddon Fitzpaine, Somerset

HOLLINGTON NURSERY
Woolton Hill, Newbury, Berkshire

IDEN CROFT NURSERIES AND
HERB FARM
Staplehurst, Kent

KNEBWORTH HOUSE
Knebworth, Hertfordshire

LEDSHAM HERB GARDEN
*The University of Liverpool Botanic Gardens
Ness, Cheshire*

LEEDS CASTLE
Maidstone, Kent

LITTLE MORETON HALL
Congleton, Cheshire

MICHELHAM PRIORY
Upper Dicker, East Sussex

MOSELEY OLD HALL
Wolverhampton, West Midlands

NETHERFIELD HERBS
Rougham, Suffolk

OAK COTTAGE HERB FARM
Nesscliffe, Shropshire

OXBURGH HALL
Swaffham, Norfolk

PETERBOROUGH CATHEDRAL
Peterborough, Cambridgeshire

QUEEN'S GARDEN AT KEW PALACE
*The Royal Botanic Gardens
Kew, London*

ROYAL HORTICULTURAL SOCIETY
Wisley, Surrey

R.T.HERBS
Kilmersdon, Somerset

SCOTNEY CASTLE
Lamberhurst, Kent

SISSINGHURST CASTLE
Sissinghurst, Kent

STOKE LACY HERB FARM
Bromyard, Hereford and Worcester

STONEACRE
Otham, Kent

TRADESCANT GARDEN
St Mary-at-Lambeth, London

TUDOR HOUSE
Southampton, Hampshire

WESTBURY COURT
Westbury-on-Severn, Gloucestershire

PHOTOGRAPHER'S NOTES AND ACKNOWLEDGMENTS

ONE CANNOT PHOTOGRAPH a hundred herb gardens in nine weeks without a great deal of help and good will from a large number of people. Throughout the time I was hardly ever indoors, except when kindly offered a meal, not even when it was raining, which in the summer of 1985 seemed to be most days. Fortunately, herb gardens being predominantly green, it is often better to work with the good yellowish overcast provided by wet weather. The illuminosity of the greens can be greatly enhanced by the right colour light that sometimes comes with rain.

With nearly all the gardens, I had to be there from 4.30 a.m., in midsummer, until 9.30 p.m., watching the light constantly and ready to shoot. It could take anything up to three days struggling against bad light and wind to get the pictures I needed of the herb gardens, and as long as seven hours to get some of the individual plant shots on film. To achieve the herb portraits I erected a black velvet cloth behind the plants to isolate them, and when necessary used a 7 by 4 ft (2 by 1.2 m) muslin sun screen to cut down the harshness of the light and yet still keep some contrast and brightness. Both of these screens were several times picked up by the wind and broken as though made of match wood, making it necessary for me to build them over again.

I took the photographs for this book with Leica cameras, R3 and R4, and would like to thank Leitz, the firm that makes them, for the loan of a 24 mm Elmarit R. lens, which gave me the widest possible view without any visible distortion, plus a 100 mm Macro-Elmar lens with bellows extension, which was absolutely vital for my herb portraits. I also made use of 35 mm, 50 mm and 90 mm lenses.

I used 100 ASA Ektachrome, as I find this film better on the greens, and I have total control with E6 processing. Kodachrome can be somewhat unpredictable in low light or deep shadow conditions, also the shadows can blacken in too much with an ugly colour caste.

I needed four filters – 05Y, 10Y, 1A, gradual ND – and the patience of Job. The 05Y and 10Y are yellow gelatine filters, which take the coldness out of a picture by cutting down the blue and accentuating the green-yellow spectrum. The 1A is used occasionally to give a warming pinkish tinge. A neutral density filter is useful on a dull day to bring the exposure of the sky closer to the exposure of the foreground by cutting down the light by a given amount while the colours and contrasts remain the same.

Finally, a tripod was used for all the pictures to steady the camera during the long exposures required by the small apertures necessary to achieve sufficient depth of field. Last, but not least, a stepladder often came in useful.

I am indebted to the owners of the gardens for their assistance and tolerance, for their willingness to allow me to camp in their gardens in my wagon for days at a time, and for giving me baths and hot meals. I would particularly like to thank the following people for the special help they gave: Rosemary and David Titterington at Iden Croft Nurseries, Simon and Judith Hopkinson at Hollington Nursery, who in the first instance allowed me to experiment with my photography and who taught me so much about herbs – I started hardly knowing the difference between Mint and Parsley – also Guy Cooper and Gordon Taylor, Rosemary Verey, Lady Salisbury, Mrs Nancy Young, the staff of the Chelsea Physic Garden, Miss B.Courtauld, Guy Acloque, Richard and Alice Taylor, Adams Hill Power Station, Paul Stocking, Mrs Galliers-Pratt, Ruth Thompson, Mr and Mrs Brackenbury, Robin Allen, Mrs Sybil Spencer, Mr and Mrs Tempest, Mrs S.M.McCosh, Chris and Sarah Braithwaite, Canon and Mrs Christie, Henry Head and Lesley Bremness.

The making of this herb book has been a fascinating experience, with a most marvellous 4,500 mile tour all over England, not twenty-five miles of it on a motorway. I met a wonderful variety of people and had the greatest of pleasure working in some of the most beautiful gardens in England.

Clive Boursnell, 1985

SELECT BIBLIOGRAPHY

Amherst, The Hon. Alicia *A History of Gardening in England*, Quaritch, London, 1895

Anderson, Frank J. *An Illustrated History of Herbals*, Columbia University Press, Guildford and New York, 1977

Blunt, Wilfrid and Raphael, Sandra *The Illustrated Herbal*, Frances Lincoln/Weidenfeld and Nicolson, London 1979; Metropolitan Museum of Art, New York, 1979

Cecil, David *The Cecils of Hatfield House*, Constable, London, 1973

Chittenden, Fred J. (Ed.) *The Dictionary of Gardening*, The Royal Horticultural Society, Clarendon Press, Oxford, 1951

Culpeper, Nicholas *The English Physitian*, 1653

Encyclopedia Britannica, Eleventh Edition, Cambridge, 1911

Fedden, Robin and Kenworthy-Brown, John *The Country House Guide*, Cape, London, 1979; Norton, New York, 1979

Gerard, John *The Herbal, or General History of Plants*, London, 1633; Dover Publications, New York, 1975

Grieve, Maude and Leyel, Hilda *A Modern Herbal*, Cape, London, 1931; Harcourt Brace, New York, 1931

Hadfield, Miles, Harling, Robert and Highton, Leonie *British Gardeners: A Biographical Dictionary*, Zwemmer/Condé Nast, London, 1980

Henrey, Blanche *British Botanical and Horticultural Literature before 1800*, Oxford University Press, Oxford, 1975

Huxley, Anthony *An Illustrated History of Gardening*, Paddington, London, 1978

Jekyll, Gertrude *Garden Ornament*, Country Life/Newnes, London, 1918; Antique Collectors Club, Woodbridge and New York, 1982

Langham, William *The Garden of Health*, 1584

Leith-Ross, Prudence *The John Tradescants*, Peter Owen, London, 1984; Kapitan-Szabo, Washington D.C., 1984

Lutyens Exhibition Catalogue, Arts Council, London, 1981

Peplow, E. and R. *Herbs and Herb Gardens of Great Britain*, Webb and Bower, Exeter, 1984; Holt, Rinehart and Winston, New York, 1984

Reader's Digest Encyclopedia of Garden Plants and Flowers, London, 1971

Rohde, Eleanour Sinclair *A Garden of Herbs*, Herbert Jenkins, London, 1932; Hale, Cushman and Flint, New York, 1936

Rohde, Eleanour Sinclair *The Story of a Garden*, Medici Society, London, 1932; Hale, Cushman and Flint, New York, 1932

Sackville-West, Vita *Vita Sackville-West's Garden Book*, Michael Joseph, London, 1968; Atheneum, New York, 1968

Scott-James, Anne *Sissinghurst: The Making of a Garden*, Michael Joseph, London, 1974

Sitwell, Sir George *On the Making of Gardens*, Duckworth, London, 1909

Stuart, Malcolm (Ed.) *The Encyclopedia of Herbs and Herbalism*, Orbis, London, 1979; Grosset and Dunlap, New York, 1979

Thomas, Graham Stuart *Gardens of the National Trust*, Weidenfeld and Nicolson, London, 1979; Mayflower, New York, 1979

Verey, Rosemary *The Scented Garden*, Michael Joseph, London, 1981; Van Nostrand Reinhold, New York, 1981

Weinreb, Ben and Hibbert, Christopher *The London Encyclopedia*, Macmillan, London, 1983; Adler and Adler, Bethesda, 1986

INDEX

(Figures in **bold** refer to main entries)

Achillea millefolium **154**
Acloque, Guy and The Hon. Mrs 23
Aconite (*Aconitum napellus*) 16, **134**
Alchemilla vulgaris **144**
Alderley, Glos: Alderley Grange 23
Allen, William Herbert 115
Allium schoenoprasum **138**
Alton, Hants: The Allen Gallery 115
Angelica (*Angelica archangelica*) **134**
Anthriscus cerefolium **137**
Apothecaries' Company 76
Apothecary's rose **135**
Artemisia abrotanum **144**; *A. dracunculus* **143**
Ashmole, Elias 79
Augusta, Princess 80
Avon, herb garden in 127

Bacon, Sir Francis: *On Gardens* 68
Baillie, The Hon. Lady 88
Barnsley, Glos: Barnsley House **19**
Basil 48, **135**
Bay 17, 100, **136**
Beaulieu, Hants: Beaulieu Abbey **112**
Bendingfeld, Sir Edmund 67
Berkshire, herb garden in 120
Birmingham, W. Mid.: Urban Herbs **35**
Borage (*Borago officinalis*) **136**
Bouncing Bet 92
Brackenbury, Mr and Mrs R. 43
Bremness, Lesley 68
Briar, Sweet 152
Bromyard, H. & W.: Stoke Lacy Herb Farm **24**

Brookes, John 104
Brownlow, Miss Margaret 24
Buckinghamshire, herb garden in 119
Bulley, Arthur 48
Burnett, Mrs Moyra 112
Burwash, E. Sussex: Bateman's **100**

Cambridge, Cambs: Emmanuel College **64**
Cambridgeshire, herb gardens in 63, 64
Cardoon 32
Carr, Graham 124
Catmint **137**
Cecil, Robert, Earl of Salisbury 75, 79, 132
Chaucer, Geoffrey, 152, 153
Cheddon Fitzpaine, Som.: Hestercombe House **131**
Chervil **137**
Cheshire, herb gardens in 47, 48
Chesterfield, Derbys: Hardwick Hall 16, **44**
Chives **138**
Chrysanthemum parthenium **142**
Claverton Manor, Avon: The American Museum **127**
Cleabury Mortimer, Shrops: Mawley Hall **27**
Clove Pink **138**
Coats, Alice 36
Codrington, John 55, 64
Colchester, Maynard 20
Comfrey 16
Congleton, Ches: Little Moreton Hall **47**
Conium maculatum **143**
Coriander (*Coriandrum sativum*) **139**

Cosby, Leics: Cosby House **39**
Cotton Lavender **139**
Courtauld, Miss J.B. 107
Culpeper, Nicholas 88, 146
Cumbria, herb garden in 60

Dandelion **140**
D'Argenville, Antoine Joseph Dezallier: *La Théorie et la Pratique du Jardinage* 67
David, Elizabeth 13
Derbyshire, herb garden in 44
Dianthus caryophyllus **138**
Digitalis 16; *D. purpurea* **142**
Dorset, herb garden in 132

Earle, Mrs C.W.: *Pot-Pourri from a Surrey Garden* 24
Elder **140**
Elecampane 96
Evelyn, John 136

Faire, Mrs Jane 39
Farnham Royal, Bucks: Farnham Royal Herbs 119
Fennel 17, **141**
Feverfew 16, **142**
Filipendula ulmaria **146**
Foeniculum vulgare **141**
Fontwell, W.Sussex: Denmans 16, **104**
Foxglove **142**

Galliers-Pratt, Mr and Mrs Anthony 27
Geranium, Peppermint **148**
Gerard, John: *The Herbal, or General History of Plants* 146
Gloucestershire, herb gardens in 19, 20, 23

Gough, Mrs Rosalind 55
Great Bedwyn, Wilts: Hillbarn House **123**
Greater London, herb gardens in 76, 79, 80, 83, 84

Hampshire, herb gardens in 108, 111, 112, 115, 116
Harrogate, N. Yorks: Harlow Car Gardens **56**
Hartley Wintney, Hants: West Green House **116**
Harvey, John: *Medieval Gardens* 63
Hatfield, Herts: Hatfield House **75**
Hemlock **143**
Henrietta Maria, Queen 79
Hereford and Worcester, herb garden in 24
Hertfordshire, herb gardens in 72, 75
Hill, William: *Gardener's Labyrinth* 36
Holland, Allan 31
Hollingbourne, Kent: Eyehorne Manor **92**
Hooper, Mrs Madge 24
Hopkinson, Judith and Simon 120
Horehound 112
Houdret, Jessica and Jeremy 119
Hussey, Christopher 99

Jekyll, Miss Gertrude 24, 72, 107, 131
Jennings, John 44
Judkyn, John 127

Kent, herb gardens in 88, 91, 92, 95, 96, 99
Kew, G. London: Queen's Garden, Royal Botanic Gardens **80**
Kilmersdon, Som.: R.T.Herbs **128**
Kipling, Rudyard 100

Knebworth, Herts: Knebworth House **72**

Lad's Love 17, **144**
Lady's Mantle **144**
Lamberhurst, Kent: Scotney Castle **99**
Landsberg, Mrs Sylvia 111
Lauderdale, 1st Duke of 84
Laurus nobilis **136**
Lavender (*Lavandula spica*) 17, **145**
Lawson, William: *The New Orchard and Garden* 39
Leamington Spa, War.: Mallory Court **31**
Leeds, W. Yorks: Abbey House Museum **51**; York Gate **52**
Lees-Milne, Mr and Mrs James 23
Leicestershire, herb garden in 39
Lemon Verbena **145**
Levisticum officinalis **146**
Linnaeus 76
Lippia citriodora **145**
London: Chelsea Physic Garden 13, **76**; Tradescant Garden, St Mary-at-Lambeth 79
Lovage **146**
Lutyens, Sir Edwin 72, 131
Lytton, Sir Edward Bulwer 72
Lytton-Cobbold, The Hon. David and Mrs 72

McCallum, Ian 127
Magnus, Albertus: *The Boke of Secretes . . .* **149**
Maidstone, Kent: Leeds Castle **88**
Marjoram, Sweet 95, 152
Meadowsweet 17, **146**
Meager, Leonard: *The Complete Gardener* 47

Mentha spicata, M. viridis **147**
Mills, Paul 47
Mint **147**
Montagu, Lord Edward 112
More, Sir Thomas 14
Mort, Jeremy 31
Mullein **147**

National Trust, The 20, 36, 44, 47, 60, 67, 84, 91, 100, 116
Nepeta cataria **137**
Nesfield, William 59
Ness, Ches: Ledsham Herb Garden, Univ. of Liverpool Botanic Gardens 48
Nesscliffe, Shrops: Oak Cottage Herb Farm 28
Nicolson, Harold 96
Norfolk, herb garden in 67
Northern Horticultural Society 56
Nottingham, Notts: Holme Pierrepont Hall 43

Ocimum basilicum **135**
Oenothera biennis **141**
Oglethorpe, James 76
Origanum majorana **152**
Otham, Kent: Stoneacre 16, **91**

Page, Russell 88
Paine, James 55
Palmer, David 87
Parish, Mr Woodbine 100
Parsley **148**

Parterres 20, 59, 67, 84
Pelargonium tomentosum **148**
Penrith, Cumbria: Acorn Bank **60**
Peplow, Mrs Elizabeth 63
Periwinkle **149**
Peterborough Cathedral, Cambs: 63
Petersfield, Hants: Butser Ancient Farm Research Project 108
Petroselinum crispum **148**
Phytolacca americana **150**
Poke Root **150**
Pratt, Dr Dallas 127
Primrose, Evening **141**

Quincunx 72

Raworth, Mrs Jenny 83
Richmond, G. London: Ham House 84
Robinson, Mrs J.H. 104
Rohde, Miss Eleanour Sinclair 24
Roper, Lanning 123
Rosa gallica officinalis **135**; *R. rubiginosa* 152
Rosemary 17, **150**
Rosmarinus officinalis **150**
Rougham, Suff.: Netherfield Herbs 68
Royal Horticultural Society 87
Rumex acetosa **151**

Sackville-West, Vita 24, 96
Sage 17, **151**; Pineapple **149**

Salisbury, Lady 75, 79, 132; *The English-woman's Garden* 132
Salvia officinalis **151**; *S. rutilans* **149**
Sambucus nigra **140**
Santolina chamaecyparissus **139**
Saponaria officinalis 92
Satureia hortensis **154**; *S. montana* **154**
Savory, Summer **154**; Winter **154**
Scolymus cardunculus 32
Shakespeare, William 91
Shrewsbury, Elizabeth Cavendish, 5th Countess of 44
Shropshire, herb gardens in 27, 28
Shugborough, Staffs: The Izaak Walton Cottage **40**
Simmons, Mr and Mrs Derek 92
Sissinghurst Castle, Kent 13, **96**
Sitwell, Sir George: *On the Making of Gardens* 17
Skipton, N. Yorks: Broughton Hall 59
Sloane, Sir Hans 76
Soapwort 92
Somerset, herb gardens in 128, 131
Sorrel **151**
Southampton, Hants: the Tudor House 111
Spearmint **147**
Spencer, Mrs Sybil **52**
Staffordshire, herb garden in 40
Staplehurst, Kent: Iden Croft Nurseries **95**
Stocking, Paul 35
Stonehouse, Rev. Walter 36

Sudbury, Suff.: Gainsborough's House 71
Suffolk, herb gardens in 68, 71
Surrey, herb garden in 87
Sussex, East: herb gardens in 100, 103
Sussex, West: herb gardens in 104, 107
Sutton Coldfield, W. Mid.: Lea Ford Cottage 32
Swaffham, Norf.: Oxburgh Hall 13, 67

Tarragon, French 31, **143**
Taraxacum officinale **140**
Taylor, Sir George 80
Taylor, Richard and Alice 128
Thomas, Graham Stuart 36
Thompson, Mrs Ruth 28
Thyer-Turner, Mr and Mrs Cecil 91
Thyme (*Thymus vulgaris*) 17, 51, **153**
Titterington, Rosemary 95
Tollemache, Sir Lyonel 84
Tradescant, John, the Elder 75, 79, 134
Tumblers Bottom Herb Farm 112, 128
Turner, William 151
Twickenham, G. London: 7 St George's Road 83

Upper Dicker, E. Sussex: Michelham Priory 103

Valerian (*Valeriana officinalis*) **153**

Verbascum thapsus **147**
Verey, David 19
Verey, Rosemary 19
Verity, Simon 19
Vinca major **149**

Walton, Izaak 40
Warwickshire, herb garden in 31
West Burton, W. Sussex: Cooke's House 107
Westbury-on-Severn, Glos: Westbury Court 20
Wetherby, N. Yorks: Stockeld Park 55
Wiltshire, herb gardens in 123, 124
Wimborne, Dorset: Cranborne Manor 132
Wisley, Surrey: Royal Horticultural Society 87
Withering, William 142
Wolverhampton, W. Mid.: Moseley Old Hall 36
Woolton Hill, Berks: Hollington Nursery 120
Wootton Rivers, Wilts: Young House 16, 124
Wyatville, Sir Jeffrey 127

Yarrow **154**
Yorkshire, North: herb gardens in 55, 56, 59
Yorkshire, West: herb gardens in 51, 52
Young, Mrs Nancy 124